LOOK UP!
A Timeline of
50 Last Days Events

DON STEWART

Look Up! A Timeline of 50 "Last Days" Events
by Don Stewart

English Versions Cited

The various English versions which we cite in this course, apart from the King James Version, all have copyrights. They are listed as follows.

TABLE OF CONTENTS

INTRODUCTION

This is the third book in our series on the study of Bible prophecy: past, present, and future.

The first book dealt with prophecies that have already been fulfilled in history. We documented that the God of the Bible has supernaturally predicted events which have now come to pass. We gave 50 specific examples of these miraculous fulfillments.

In our second book, *25 Signs We Are Near the End*, we detailed a number of Biblical predictions as to what our world will be like as we approach the time of the end. We discovered the remarkable fulfillments of many of the predictions that Scripture has made, as well as the stage being set of those predictions that have not yet come to pass.

In this third book, *Look Up! A Timeline of 50 "Last Days" Events,* we will now present a basic timeline of 50 major events that Scripture says will take place in the future.

Our title is derived from a statement of Jesus in Luke 21:28. He said:

When you begin to see these things take place, look up, and lift up your head, for your redemption draws nigh.

Since the stage is now being set for these predictions to become a reality, it is an exciting time to examine these "last days" events.

SOME PRELIMINARY MATTERS

Before we examine the timeline of 50 of the events that the Bible predicts will take place in the "last days," there are a couple of preliminary issues that we must deal with.

CHRISTIANS HAVE DIFFERENT VIEWS ON THIS SUBJECT

To begin with, most Bible-believers understand that Scripture predicts that certain events will take place in the future. This book will concentrate on the main events that are predicted to occur.

However, since we are dealing with the future, there is some question as to the exact sequence of these events. In fact, we recognize that there are Christians who do not believe that many of these events will literally occur. In other words, they are thought to be merely symbolic.

In our companion book, *25 Signs We Are Near the End*, we spent some time in one of our appendices explaining why we reject this position. Consequently, what we went over in that book will be the stance of this book—that we are talking about genuine events that will, literally, occur in the future.

Yet, even for those who do believe that these events will literally occur in the future, there is still some disagreement as to the precise order of these coming events.

For example, we have documented in our book *The Rapture* that there are seven different views as to the timing, or even the fact, that the rapture will take place.

In the same way, Christians view the events that we will discuss in this book, such as those recorded in the Book of Revelation, in a number of different sequences.

While we will be giving one possible sequence of events, the important thing to note is that these events will literally occur at some time in the future.

Before we look at the specific events that the Bible predicts will happen, we must first examine the "outline of history" that the Lord has given to us.

THE BASIC OUTLINE OF BIBLE HISTORY (DANIEL 9:24-27)

We are fortunate that the Lord has given us the outline of history in the 9th chapter of the Book of Daniel. Indeed, in four verses, we can have a general understanding of God's dealings in the past, the present, and in the future. Consequently, it is absolutely crucial that we understand this passage.

THE BACKGROUND

The background of this chapter is the end of the seventy-year Babylonian captivity. The captivity began in 606 B.C. In reading the Book of Jeremiah, Daniel realized that the specified time of the captivity, seventy years, was about over.

Through the angel Gabriel, the Lord gave the prophecy of the "seventy sevens." The Hebrew word "heptad" translated as "seven" can refer to seven "days," "weeks," "months" or "years." The fact that this prophecy was given to Daniel in the context of the seventy-year Babylonian captivity, makes it clear that "years" are in view here.

THE THREE PROPHETIC PERIODS

God outlined to Daniel three prophetic periods for the history of Israel. They are recorded in the following verses:

> "Seventy 'sevens' are decreed for your people and your holy city to finish transgression, to put an end to sin, to atone for wickedness, to bring in everlasting righteousness, to seal up vision and prophecy and to anoint the Most Holy Place. "Know and understand this: From the time the word goes out to restore and rebuild Jerusalem until the Anointed One, the ruler, comes, there will be seven 'sevens,' and sixty-two 'sevens.' It will be rebuilt with streets and a trench, but in times of trouble. After the sixty-two 'sevens,' the Anointed One will be put to death and will have nothing. The people of the ruler who will come will destroy the city and the sanctuary. The end will come like a flood: War will continue until the end, and desolations have been decreed. He will confirm a covenant with many for one 'seven.' In the middle of the 'seven' he will put an end to sacrifice and offering. And at the temple he will set up an abomination that causes desolation, until the end that is decreed is poured out on him (Daniel 9:24-27 NIV).

Simply stated, the Lord divided the prophetic future into three different time periods.

The first period consists of four hundred and eighty-three years: a time period of "seven sevens" (forty-nine years) plus "sixty-two sevens" (four hundred thirty-four years). They add up to four hundred and eighty-three years.

This prophetic time period would begin with the issue of a commandment for the rebuilding of the city and the walls of Jerusalem, and would end with the presentation of the Messiah as the King of the Jews.

The second period is the present age in which we are living—the church age. It is an indefinite period of time which began immediately upon the close of the first, and will end with the resurrection of the dead "in Christ" and the catching up in the air of living believers—the rapture of the church. We will explain these two events later.

The third is a brief period of only seven years. Among other things, it is known as the "Seventieth Week of Daniel," or the "Time of Jacob's Trouble." It begins on the day when the final Antichrist, the last Gentile world ruler, makes, or forces, a seven-year covenant with the majority of the Jewish nation. This period will be a time of judgment for the people living upon the earth.

It's during this last seven-year period that the Lord will resume His dealings with the Jews. This period will end with the Second Coming of Jesus Christ to the earth to set up His everlasting kingdom.

One of Daniel's three prophetic periods has now passed. We are presently in the second period. As we mentioned, it is an interval of unknown time.

SUMMARIZING DANIEL 9
WE CAN SUMMARIZE THESE FOUR VERSES IN DANIEL AS FOLLOWS:

The prophetic time clock was to start at a time future to Daniel, who was writing in about 540 B.C. When a certain commandment would be given for the people to return to Jerusalem, and to rebuild the city and the walls, there would be a total of483 years until the Messiah arrives.

THE CLOCK STOPS

After the 483 years is complete, the prophetic clock stops. There is then an interval of unknown time. During this interval, the Messiah is killed, and the city of Jerusalem and the Temple are destroyed.

THE CLOCK RESTARTS

The prophetic clock will then restart when a certain seven-year covenant, or agreement, is made between this Final Antichrist, the last Gentile world ruler, and the Jewish people. The agreement is "confirmed" or "forced upon" the Jewish people at that time.

In sum, we are in the second of three phases of prophetic history. The first lasted for four hundred and eighty-three years. This second phase is of an unknown length. The third phase begins when a seven-year agreement is signed between the final Antichrist and the nation of Israel. At the end of the seven years, Jesus Christ returns to the earth!

With this as our basic outline of history, let us now look at a timeline of fifty events that Scripture predicts will happen in the "last days."

The Resurrection of the Dead "in Christ" (1 Thessalonians 4:16)

The first event on the prophetic calendar, according to our view of the time frame of the "last days," is the resurrection of the dead "in Christ." There are a few things which we should note as we explain this coming event.

IT IS NOT A RESURRECTION OF EVERY BELIEVER FROM THE BEGINNING

First, it is the resurrection of a particular group of people—the dead "in Christ." This is a technical term for all those who have died as believers in Jesus as the Messiah during this present age. This age began at the Day of Pentecost when the Holy Spirit fell upon the disciples of Jesus in Jerusalem (Acts 2). This age will end with the resurrection of the dead "in Christ."

THE OLD TESTAMENT SAINTS WILL BE RAISED LATER

Therefore, the Old Testament saints will not be raised at this time. This event will take place at the Second Coming of Jesus Christ. This is another of the future events that we will discuss.

THE TRIBULATION SAINTS WILL ALSO BE RAISED AT THE SECOND COMING

In addition, those who come to believe in Christ, and who die after the resurrection of the dead "in Christ," will also be raised at the Second Coming. They are known as the "tribulation saints." We will also have more to say about them later.

THE RESURRECTION OF THOSE DEAD "IN CHRIST"

The Bible speaks of this event, the resurrection of the New Testament believers, as follows:

> For the Lord himself will come down from heaven, with a loud command, with the voice of the archangel and with the trumpet call of God, and the dead in Christ will rise first (1 Thessalonians 4:16 NIV).

We are told that the Lord will leave the glory of heaven, with a loud cry, with the voice of an archangel, and with a trumpet call from the Lord. Then those who have died "in Christ" will rise first.

The Apostle Paul wrote about a specific order of these future events:

> For since death came through a man, the resurrection of the dead comes also through a man. For as in Adam all die, so in Christ all will be made alive. But each in turn: Christ, the firstfruits; then, when he comes, those who belong to him (1 Corinthians 15:21-23 NIV).

We should observe that Paul said that each will be raised "in turn" or "in their own order." Christ was raised first—the firstfruits. Next, when He returns at this particular time, seven years before His Second Coming, the New Testament believers will be raised from the dead—the dead "in Christ."

Since this specific term, the dead "in Christ," is used exclusively in the Bible of those who have become believers in the New Testament age, it refers to a specific group of people. In other words, it is not talking about those who lived before the time of Christ, or those who will believe in Him after this event takes place.

THIS SEQUENCE IS DISPUTED BY SOME CHRISTIANS

The resurrection of the dead "in Christ" is the next event to take place on the prophetic calendar in our view. However, not everyone agrees with this sequence. There are good Christians who believe that the resurrection of all of the believing dead will occur at the same time. In other words, there is a resurrection "day" where everyone is raised at once.

We have dealt with this objection in detail in our book *Resurrection and Judgment*. Basically, we contend that the Scriptures make a distinction between three groups of believers: The Old Testament saints, those who believe after Christ came into the world, and those who will believe after the church age is over. While they are all raised from the dead, they are not all raised at the same time.

Therefore, in conclusion, the next great event on the prophetic calendar is the resurrection of the believers who have died "in Christ."

Furthermore, this particular event is linked with the next one in our prophetic timeline—the rapture of the church.

EVENT 2

The Resurrection of the Dead "in Christ"
(1 Thessalonians 4:16)

At the same time the dead "in Christ" are raised, another event takes place. This is the "catching up" of the living believers. This is also known as the "rapture of the church."

WHAT DO WE MEAN BY THE "RAPTURE OF THE CHURCH?"

The doctrine of the rapture of the church can be simply stated as follows: At some future time, the *genuine* believers in Jesus Christ—not merely people who have a church membership or affiliation—will be caught up to meet Him in the air when He descends from heaven. Those Christians who are alive will be instantaneously changed from their mortal bodies into immortal bodies, from corruptible bodies to incorruptible bodies.

Immediately before this happens, the believers who have died "in Christ" will be raised from the graves into their new bodies where they, too, will be with the Lord. This is the "blessed hope" of the true believers in Jesus.

WHERE DO WE GET THE TERM RAPTURE?

The English term *rapture* is derived from the Latin Vulgate translation of the New Testament. The Latin verb *rapere* is a translation of the Greek word *harpadzo* which has the meaning of "to be caught up."

It is the word used in one of the main passages describing this event (1 Thessalonians 4:17). In this verse, the believers are promised to be "caught up" to be with the Lord (Greek *harpadzo*, Latin *rapere*). Hence, the English word "rapture" comes to us by way of the Greek and the Latin.

We should note that while *rapere* is a verb meaning "to be caught up," this word has been turned into a noun, "the rapture." Thus, "the rapture" has become the popular way to portray this predicted "catching away" of believers.

Scripture explains it in this manner:

> After that, [the resurrection of the dead in Christ] we who are still alive and are left will be caught up together with them in the clouds to meet the Lord in the air. And so we will be with the Lord forever. Therefore encourage one another with these words (1 Thessalonians 4:17, 18 NIV).

Immediately after the dead in Christ are raised, the living believers are then caught up to meet the Lord in the air.

In another place, Paul explained it in this manner:

> Listen, I tell you a mystery: We will not all sleep, but we will all be changed—in a flash, in the twinkling of an eye, at the last trumpet. For the trumpet will sound, the dead will be raised imperishable, and we will be changed. For the perishable must clothe itself with the imperishable, and the mortal with immortality. When the perishable has been clothed with the imperishable, and the mortal with immortality, then the saying that is written will come true: "Death has been swallowed up in victory." "Where, O death, is your victory? Where, O death, is your sting?" The sting of death is sin, and the power of sin is the law. But thanks be to God! He gives us the victory through our Lord Jesus Christ. Therefore,

my dear brothers and sisters, stand firm. Let nothing move you. Always give yourselves fully to the work of the Lord, because you know that your labor in the Lord is not in vain (1 Corinthians 15:51-58 NIV).

This is a further explanation of what will transpire.

WHAT THE BIBLE SAYS WILL TAKE PLACE

When we put these various passages together, we find that a number of things will occur at the time of the rapture of the church.

THE DEAD IN CHRIST RISE FIRST, THEN THE LIVING ARE CAUGHT UP

As we observed in our previous event, those who have died "in Christ" will be raised first. Immediately after this takes place the living believers will be caught up to meet the Lord in the air to be with those who have died "in Christ."

As the living believers are being caught up, they are changed from mortal to immortal, from a corruptible body to an incorruptible one. The result is that all believers in Jesus Christ, those who have died as well as those who are alive, will all receive a glorified body at that time.

THE NEW BODY

The glorified body will be like that of the Lord Jesus after He rose from the dead. John wrote:

Dear friends, now we are children of God, and what we will be has not yet been made known. But we know that when Christ appears, we shall be like him, for we shall see him as he is (1 John 3:2 NIV).

The promise of Scripture is that, someday, all believers will be like Him in a resurrected, or a glorified, body.

THE VARIOUS VIEWS OF THE RAPTURE

As we mentioned, there are different views that believers hold with respect to this event.

Some do not believe it will literally occur. In other words, they interpret these passages as being merely symbolic—not meant to be understood as an actual event that will occur. However, of those who see the passages as symbolic, nobody seems to agree as to exactly what they are symbolic of!

Others believe the rapture will occur in stages where believers will be caught up at various times during the last seven-year period. This is known as the "Partial Rapture Theory."

There is also the belief that this event will take place before the final seven-year period begins—"the 70th week of Daniel." Among other things, this is known as the "Pre-Tribulation Rapture View." This is the view that we hold.

We also have the belief, called the "Mid-Tribulation View," that holds that this event occurs in the middle of the coming seven-year period.

Two other views, with respect to the timing of this event, are the "Pre-Wrath Rapture View" and the "Post-Tribulation Rapture View." Pre-Wrath holds that this event takes place about five and one-half years into the final seven-year period, while the Post-Tribulation theory believes that it occurs at the very end—at the coming of Christ.

One other view says that while the Bible teaches that such an event will occur, there is insufficient information given to us in Scripture for us to know the exact timing of the rapture of the church.

As mentioned, we have dealt with each of these theories in our book *The Rapture* where we concluded that the Pre-Tribulation Rapture view is the one position that can best explain all the evidence, while each of the other theories have unsolvable problems.

Having said that, there are good Bible-believing people who hold to each of these views. Therefore, while we may disagree with the other positions, we hold our view with love towards all as well as with much humility.

With these two great events, the resurrection of the dead "in Christ" and the catching up of living believers, the "rapture of the church," will officially end the church age.

EVENT 3

The Judgment Seat of Christ
(2 Corinthians 5:10)

This next event takes place in heaven. It will affect all of those who have believed in Jesus Christ during this present church age.

Greek, like English, uses the word "judge" in two senses. One sense is condemnation, while the other sense is the giving out of rewards. The Bible says unbelievers will be judged in the first sense. In other words, it speaks of their condemnation.

On the other hand, believers will be judged in a different sense—rewards. The following observations need to be made:

THERE IS A JUDGMENT SEAT OF GOD FOR BELIEVERS

The Bible speaks of a special judgment that God will hold for believers only. It is known as the "judgment seat of Christ" or the "judgment seat of God." Writing to believers, Paul stated the following:

> For we must all appear before the judgment seat of Christ, so that each of us may receive what is due us for the things done while in the body, whether good or bad (2 Corinthians 5:10 NIV).

All believers will stand before God and be individually judged. According to Paul, the purpose of this judgment is to receive rewards.

Paul also wrote to the Romans about this judgment seat of God. He said each of us who have believed in Jesus will stand before Him:

> Why do you pass judgment on your brother? Or you, why do you despise your brother? For we will all stand before the judgment seat of God (Romans 14:10 ESV).

Every believer will one day stand in His presence—before God's judgment seat.

THE JUDGMENT SEAT: THE BEMA

The judgment seat is known as the "bema." This Greek word is also translated "court" or "tribunal." The word could refer to a public judgment place, as in the case with Pontius Pilate and Jesus. We read of this kind of "judge's seat" in the Gospel of John:

> When Pilate heard this, he brought Jesus out and sat down on the judge's seat [bema] at a place known as the Stone Pavement (which in Aramaic is Gabbatha) (John 19:13 NIV).

Pilate sat down on the bema—the judge's seat.

Later the Apostle Paul appeared before Festus the governor.

> Festus stayed in Jerusalem for eight or ten more days before going to Caesarea. Then the next day he took his place as judge [bema] and had Paul brought into court (Acts 25:6 NIV).

The phrase translated "took his place as judge" is a Greek phrase, which literally translated, says "sitting upon the bema."

THE REWARD SEAT

However, the bema seat was not only used to judge suspected criminals, it was also used as a place to present rewards. In the large Olympic arenas in the ancient world there was an elevated seat on which the judge of the contest sat. After the contest was over, those who were successful in their competition would assemble before the bema to receive their rewards or crowns.

Therefore, in this instance, the bema was not a judicial bench where someone was condemned for their wrongdoings, but rather it was a reward seat.

OUR SINS HAVE ALREADY BEEN JUDGED

Likewise, the "Judgment Seat of Christ" is not a judicial bench where believers are condemned for their sins. Our sins have already been entirely paid for by Jesus Christ on the cross of Calvary. There is no more condemnation for those of us who are in Christ Jesus. The judgment of the sins of believers is a thing of the past.

Consequently, the Judgment Seat of Christ is actually the "Reward Seat." In fact, the Christian life is compared to a race which all believers run to win an eternal prize. Paul wrote:

> Don't you realize that in a race everyone runs, but only one person gets the prize? So run to win! All athletes are disciplined in their training. They do it to win a prize that will fade away, but we do it for an eternal prize. So I run with purpose in every step . . . (1 Corinthians 9:24-26 NLT).

Jesus Christ is the Judge or Rewarder of all Christians. The good news is that there is not merely one winner in the race which believers are running. Indeed, because we belong to Him we are all winners and we all will be rewarded!

WHAT WILL HAPPEN AT THE JUDGMENT SEAT?

What will happen at this judgment seat of God? Who will be judged?

The Scriptures have the following to say:

> Only New Testament Believers Will Be Judged (The Church)

The participants in the judgment seat of Christ, or the judgment seat of God, are members of the New Testament church. These are people who have trusted Jesus Christ as their Savior from the Day of Pentecost, when the church began, until the coming of Christ for His bride—the rapture of the church. It does not include the Old Testament believers. They will have a separate time of judgment and reward.

Paul made it clear that this judgment is only for those have built their foundation on Jesus Christ. He wrote the following to the Corinthians:

> For no one can lay any other foundation than what has been laid down. That foundation is Jesus Christ . . . Each one's work will become obvious. For the day will disclose it, because it will be revealed by fire; the fire will test the quality of each one's work. If anyone's work that he has built survives, he will receive a reward. If anyone's work is burned up, he will experience loss, but he himself will be saved—but only as through fire (1 Corinthians 3:11,13-15 CSB).

Only believers in Christ receive rewards from God. Unbelievers, by definition, cannot do anything that pleases God. They will not receive any rewards, only condemnation.

2. IT WILL OCCUR BEFORE THE SECOND COMING OF CHRIST

The judging of New Testament believers will occur after the rapture of the church, but before the Second Coming of Christ to the earth.

In the Book of Revelation, we read the following:

> Let us be glad, rejoice, and give him glory, because the marriage of the Lamb has come, and his bride has prepared herself. She was given fine linen to wear, bright and pure. For the fine linen represents the righteous acts of the saints (Revelation 19:7,8 CSB).

This is a picture of the believers before the Second Coming of Jesus Christ. We are told that the bride is clothed with righteous deeds. The church, therefore, has already been at the judgment seat of Christ because they are ready for the groom when He comes. Hence, the judgment, or evaluation, takes place sometime before the Second Coming of Christ.

3. BELIEVERS ARE NOT JUDGED FOR THEIR SIN AT THE JUDGMENT SEAT

Again, it is important to realize that this is not a judgment to determine who will enter heaven. The sins of believers will not be an issue at the judgment seat of Christ. Indeed, they have already been forgiven once-and -for-all. The Bible says:

> He doesn't punish us as our sins deserve. How great is God's love for all who worship him? Greater than the distance between heaven and earth! How far has the LORD taken our sins from us? Farther than the distance from east to west! (Psalm 103:10-12 CEV).

As far as the east is from the west, so are our sins from us!

This is taught elsewhere. The prophet Micah wrote that our sins have been thrown into the depths of the ocean. He said:

> Once again you will have compassion on us. You will trample our sins under your feet and throw them into the depths of the ocean! (Micah 7:19 NLT).

Clearly, sin has already been judged. The judgment seat of Christ is for rewards.

THE DESTINY OF THE CHRISTIAN HAS BEEN SETTLED

With the death of Jesus Christ on the cross of Calvary, the destiny of the Christian has been once-and-for-all settled. There is no condemnation for those who have believed in Christ. Paul wrote:

Therefore, no condemnation now exists for those in Christ Jesus (Romans 8:1 CSB).

Those who have believed in Jesus will not be condemned. The penalty for our sins has already been paid for.

THE PRICE HAS BEEN PAID FOR OUR SIN

The message of the New Testament is that Jesus Christ has paid the price for our sins. Peter wrote about this. He said:

> He himself bore our sins in his body on the cross, so that we might die to sins and live for righteousness; by his wounds you have been healed (1 Peter 2:24 NIV).

Since He has paid for our sins, we do not have to suffer for them. He has paid the price in full. There is nothing we can do to add to what He has done.

4. THE BELIEVERS WILL RECEIVE THEIR REWARDS AT THE JUDGMENT SEAT

Consequently, the judgment seat of Christ is not designed to punish believers, but rather to reward them for their faithful service. All of us will give an account of what we have done after trusting Christ as Savior.

Therefore, the judgment seat of Christ is a judgment of believer's works *after* salvation. Paul gave this analogy:

> According to the grace of God given to me, like a skilled master builder I laid a foundation, and someone else is building upon it. Let each one take care how he builds upon it. For no one can lay a foundation other than that which is laid, which is Jesus Christ. Now if anyone builds on the foundation with gold, silver, precious stones, wood, hay, straw—each one's work will become manifest, for the Day will disclose it, because it will be revealed by fire, and the fire

will test what sort of work each one has done (1 Corinthians 3:10-13 ESV).

Therefore, the works performed after a person becomes a Christian will be examined. The good works will be separated from the bad. Rewards will be given for these good works.

ALL OF OUR ACTIONS WILL BE EXAMINED

The Bible says that God will reward the actions of believers. The psalmist wrote about the Lord rewarding His people:

> And that you, O Lord, are loving. Surely you will reward each person according to what he has done (Psalm 62:12 NIV).

God has promised to reward those who trust in Him. The rewards will be based upon our actions as believers in Christ.

The Apostle Paul wrote about the rewards of the Lord. He said the following to the Ephesians about what we will receive for the good which we do:

> Serve with a good attitude, as to the Lord and not to people, knowing that whatever good each one does, slave or free, he will receive this back from the Lord (Ephesians 6:7,8 CSB).

Every single thing that we have done will be evaluated, and the good will be rewarded.

5. SOME WILL SUFFER LOSS OF THEIR REWARD

Not everyone will receive the same reward when believers are gathered together for evaluation. Indeed, we are told that at the judgment seat of Jesus Christ, there will be those who suffer loss. Paul made this clear to the Corinthians. He said:

If his work is burned up, he will suffer the loss. However, he will be saved, though it will be like going through a fire (1 Corinthians 3:15 God's Word).

Some people will lose their heavenly reward. Again, they will not lose heaven itself, merely the reward in heaven.

Paul wrote elsewhere about suffering loss as a believer in Christ. In writing to the Corinthians, he made the following comparison:

Do you not know that in a race all the runners run, but only one receives the prize? So run that you may obtain it. Every athlete exercises self-control in all things. They do it to receive a perishable wreath, but we an imperishable. So I do not run aimlessly; I do not box as one beating the air. But I discipline my body and keep it under control, lest after preaching to others I myself should be disqualified (1 Corinthians 9:24-27 ESV).

Paul gave the analogy of running a race. He did not want to be disqualified from the race. Indeed, he wanted to win. Consequently, he practiced self-control.

We emphasize that the idea of being disqualified has nothing to do with the loss of salvation—Paul was concerned with the loss of reward. His salvation was eternally secure.

THE REWARDS WILL BE OF OUR OWN MAKING

To sum up, the rewards we receive in heaven will be of our own making. While salvation is a free gift, rewards are earned. In fact, the Bible says that the wise will shine. We read in Daniel:

Those who are wise will shine like the brightness of the heavens, and those who lead many to righteousness, like the stars for ever and ever (Daniel 12:3 NIV).

Our garments will shine, but they will not all shine the same. While every believer is at the Wedding Feast of Christ and dressed in white garments, we will not all be dressed the same or rewarded the same. It will depend upon how faithful we have been to the ministry the Lord has given to each of us. Therefore, as we live each day, each of us is making our own garments for that future day of reward.

SOME PEOPLE HAVE A DIFFERENT VIEW OF THE JUDGMENT SEAT OF CHRIST

We must note that not all Christians believe the judgment seat of Christ will be limited to New Testament believers. Many Christians hold the view that this is part of one general judgment of all humanity—not a number of separate judgments. They believe that the Bible teaches that all humanity, not just New Testament Christians, will be judged at the same time. They equate this judgment with the "Judgment of the Nations" spoken of in Matthew 25:31-46 and the "Great White Throne Judgment" in Revelation 20:10-15.

There are two views as to when this general judgment of all humanity will occur. One view sees it occurring at the Second Coming of Christ, while the other view has it happening at the end of Christ's thousand-year reign upon the earth—the Millennium. We look at these questions in detail in our book *Resurrection and Judgment*.

EVENT 4

The Day of the Lord
(1 Thessalonians 5:2, 3)

In both testaments, we encounter the phrase "the day of the Lord." What does it refer to? Is it one particular day or a period of time?

IT REFERS TO A SPECIAL TIME IN HISTORY

The "day of the Lord" refers of a specific time in the future when the Lord Himself will divinely intervene in our world in a number of direct ways. Included under the expression is a large group of prophetic events predicted in both the Old and the New Testaments.

THE EXTENT OF THE DAY OF THE LORD

The "day of the Lord" will begin with the "Seventieth week of Daniel," the "Great Tribulation," and will continue all the way through the Millennium—the thousand-year reign of Jesus Christ upon the earth. Therefore, it contains both judgment, in the Tribulation period, as well as blessings, in the Millennium.

Please note that the Great Tribulation is technically the "second half" of the last seven-year period (Matthew 24:21); but, for convenience sake, we will call the entire period "the Great Tribulation," as it is popularly called.

THE GREAT TRIBULATION IS PART OF THE DAY OF THE LORD

We find that Jesus used the phrase the "Great Tribulation" to describe what would take place in the "day of the Lord." He said:

> For then there will be great distress, unequaled from the beginning of the world until now—and never to be equaled again (Matthew 24:21 NIV).

This is a reference to a couple of Old Testament passages which speak of this coming "day of the Lord." For example, we read in Jeremiah:

> How awful that day will be! No other will be like it. It will be a time of trouble for Jacob, but he will be saved out of it (Jeremiah 30:7 NIV)

Daniel wrote of this:

> At that time shall arise Michael, the great prince who has charge of your people. And there shall be a time of trouble, such as never has been since there was a nation till that time (Daniel 12:1 ESV).

The prophet Joel also wrote of this coming time period:

> Blow the trumpet in Zion; sound the alarm on my holy hill. Let all who live in the land tremble, for the day of the Lord is coming. It is close at hand—a day of darkness and gloom, a day of clouds and blackness (Joel 2:1,2 NIV).

IT INCLUDES THE SECOND COMING OF CHRIST

The phrase "the day of the Lord" also refers to the Second Coming of Christ since it includes all events between the Seventieth Week of Daniel, the Great Tribulation, through the Millennium—the thousand-year reign of Christ upon the earth.

IT WILL ARRIVE UNEXPECTEDLY

For the people living on the earth at this time, the day of the Lord will arrive unexpectedly. In fact, Paul said it will come "like a thief:"

> For you yourselves know very well that the day of the Lord will come just like a thief in the night. When they say, "Peace and security," then sudden destruction will come upon them, like labor pains on a pregnant woman, and they will not escape (1 Thessalonians 5:2,3 CSB).

The meaning of the term "like a thief" emphasizes that it will surprise people.

THE DAY OF THE LORD: THE EVENING AND THEN THE MORNING

The day of the Lord looks forward to both judgment as well as restoration. Just as the Bible depicts a "day" with two parts, the evening and the morning, so the day of the Lord has two parts. First, the evening, the time of the pouring out of God's judgment during the Great Tribulation period. Then, the morning, which is the one-thousand-year reign of Messiah Jesus on this earth, the Millennium.

In sum, the "Day of the Lord" is an extended period of time starting with the "Seventieth Week of Daniel" and continuing through the Second Coming of Jesus Christ, as well as throughout the entire Millennium.

HOW DOES THIS RELATE TO THE RAPTURE OF THE CHURCH?

Since the "Day of the Lord" begins with the start of the "Seventieth Week of Daniel," the obvious question that arises is this: How does this relate to the rapture of the church. As we mentioned in Event 2, we believe the rapture of the church takes place before the "Seventieth Week of Daniel." This has caused some to teach that the "Day of the Lord" actually starts with the rapture of the church.

Whatever the case may be, the time when the Lord will pour out His wrath upon the world is coincident with the rapture and the beginning of the last seven-year period, the Great Tribulation.

The Day of Christ
(Philippians 2:16)

In a number of places in the New Testament we read of the "day of Christ" or the "day of Jesus Christ." What exactly does this mean? Is this the same as the "day of the Lord?"

THE CONTRASTS BETWEEN THE DAY OF THE LORD AND THE DAY OF CHRIST

While the expression is similar to the "day of the Lord," there is a tremendous contrast between the two. We can list some of these differences as follows:

THE NEW TESTAMENT VERSUS THE ENTIRE BIBLE

For one thing, the day of the Lord is mentioned in both testaments while the day of Christ is limited to the New Testament.

JUDGMENT VERSUS BLESSING

Furthermore, in the day of the Lord we have the emphasis upon God's judgment. Indeed, there are a number of ominous warnings connected with this time period.

The day of Christ, on the other hand, has to do with the church being gathered to Christ, the "rapture of the church," as well as the time of reward for the believer, the "judgment seat of Christ."

In sum, the day of Jesus Christ refers to the culmination of the work of the Lord Jesus in the salvation of the believer. Indeed, the phrase points to the time when Christ will return for His own and then reward them for their faithfulness to Him. Since we have already considered each of these two future events (Event 2 and Event 3), we will merely make a few observations about this future time.

THERE ARE MANY REFERENCE TO THIS DAY

There are about twenty references to this "day of Christ" in the New Testament. In other words, it is not an obscure teaching. In fact, it is highlighted by Scripture.

For example, in the Book of Philippians we read:

> Do everything without grumbling or arguing, so that you may be blameless and pure, children of God without blemish though you live in a crooked and perverse society, in which you shine as lights in the world by holding on to the word of life so that on the day of Christ I will have a reason to boast that I did not run in vain nor labor in vain (Philippians 2:14-16 NET).

Paul wanted the Philippians to continue serving the Lord so that, on the "day of Christ," he would have a reason to boast.

In sum, it is important that we keep the distinction between the "day of the Lord" and the "day of Christ." The main emphasis on the "day of the Lord" is God's judgment against a Christ-rejecting humanity, though it does include the blessings associated with the return of Christ.

On the other hand, the "day of Christ" is exclusively a time of blessing for those who have trusted Jesus Christ as their Savior.

The Ezekiel 38, 39 Invasion

One of the major events that is yet to take place is the invasion of Israel by certain nations as recorded in Ezekiel 38,39. There are so many aspects to this event that we will not be able to cover everything. Hence, we will just mention some of the highlights here. Eventually, we plan to do an entire book on the subject.

IS IT LITERAL OR SYMBOLIC?

Before we look at what the Scripture says will take place, we will first explain why we believe that this is a literal battle rather than a symbolic battle. We do this because many Bible commentators see this as a symbolic event. In other words, they believe that we are not to look for any literal fulfillment in the past or in the future.

Why, then, should we consider these chapters to be predicting actual events that will take place?

THERE WAS LITERAL FULFILLMENT IN THE PAST OF OTHER PROPHECIES BY EZEKIEL

To begin with, we find that the past predictions that Ezekiel, the "prophet," made, have all been literally fulfilled! Consequently, if this is the case with the other prophecies recorded in his writings, then why should we expect these events listed in Chapters 38 and 39 not to be fulfilled in a literal manner?

In fact, it would be strange for us to assume that they would be fulfilled in any other manner since we have the precedent in previous chapters of an exact fulfillment.

THERE IS NOTHING IN THESE CHAPTERS WHICH DEMANDS A SYMBOLIC FULFILLMENT

Furthermore, as we closely examine these chapters, we find nothing that causes us to interpret them figuratively. This is crucial. Usually there are obvious clues as to why a passage, or certain parts of it, is to be understood symbolically. Though these chapters do use symbolic language, and speak of tremendous signs in the heavens, this is not inconsistent of what we read elsewhere in Scripture which describes actual phenomena that occurred or that will occur.

THERE ARE MANY SPECIFIC DETAILS IN THESE CHAPTERS

In addition, there are too many details in these chapters that argue for a literal fulfillment. If symbolic, it is hard to understand why we have so many minute details. In fact, the natural way of understanding Ezekiel 38 and 39 is that of an invasion of the Promised Land that will literally be thwarted by God Himself.

SYMBOLIC INTERPRETERS DO NOT COME TO THE SAME CONCLUSIONS AS TO WHAT IT MEANS

If Ezekiel 38,39 is meant to be symbolic, then we must the ask the question, "Symbolic of what?" It seems interpreters are all over the map in attempting to tell us what these chapters are symbolic of. The fact that we have so many diverse interpretations of what these chapters are supposed to mean, if not understood literally, provides further reason to reject the idea of symbolic interpretation.

In sum, we conclude that what we have in these two chapters is a prediction of a future attempted invasion of the Promised Land by various nations, coming from a variety of different directions.

THERE IS ALSO THE QUESTION OF TIMING

Once we conclude that the events listed in Ezekiel 38,39 are to be interpreted literally, there is another question that must be considered. Like the previous events which we have considered, events one through three, there are different views as to when this particular invasion will occur. In addition, there are some Bible commentators who argue that this invasion has already taken place in the past.

Our view is that it is an event that is still future. Indeed, there is nothing that has taken place in the past that remotely suggests that it has already taken place. Furthermore, as we shall note, we are specifically told that this invasion will take place "at the time of the end."

THE INVASION OCCURS IN THE LAST DAYS

The fact that this event is still future, and that it will take place at the time of the end, is emphasized for us in Ezekiel 38:8. It reads as follows:

> After many days you will be summoned; in the latter years you
> will come to a land restored from the ravages of war, with many
> peoples gathered on the mountains of Israel that had long been
> in ruins. Its people were brought out from the peoples, and all
> of them will be living securely (Ezekiel 38:8 NET).

Since twice in this verse we have the terms "after many days," and "in the latter years," it is an indication that this invasion will take place at the time of the end. Indeed, when the specifics of this predicted event are examined, it will become clear that we are dealing with something that has never occurred in the past.

EXACTLY WHEN IN THE FUTURE IS MUCH DEBATED

However, precisely when it will take place in the future is a difficult question to answer. To the point, there are at least ten different views as to when it will occur! We can briefly list them as follows:

OPTION 1: IT WILL HAPPEN SOMETIME DURING THE CHURCH AGE, LIKELY AT THE END

This position sees the invasion taking place during the church age before the beginning of the Seventieth Week of Daniel—the final seven-year period before Jesus Christ returns to the earth to set up His kingdom (Daniel 9:24-27). Those who hold this position often view it occurring during the very end of the church age, but this is not always the case.

OPTION 2: THE BATTLE OCCURS BEFORE THE RAPTURE OF THE CHURCH AND THE GREAT TRIBULATION

This view is similar to the previous one. The battle will happen during the church age, but at the very extreme end. In other words, it will take place almost simultaneously with the rapture of the church and the beginning of the seventieth week of Daniel, the Great Tribulation.

The sequence is usually explained in this manner: the invasion begins, the rapture of the church takes place immediately afterward, and then the Great Tribulation immediately follows.

OPTION 3: IT OCCURS AFTER THE RAPTURE, BEFORE THE 70TH WEEK OF DANIEL (THE GREAT TRIBULATION)

This view sees the invasion taking place after the rapture of the church, but before the Great Tribulation, the Seventieth week of Daniel, begins. It is contended that there may be a large time gap between the rapture of the church and the start of the final seven-year period—the Great Tribulation. This view says that that interval may be days, weeks, months or even years between the rapture of the church and the beginning of the Great Tribulation. The Ezekiel 38,39 invasion takes places during this interval.

OPTION 4: IT TAKES PLACE EARLY IN THE GREAT TRIBULATION, AFTER THE RAPTURE

Another view holds that the rapture of the church has taken place, and the Great Tribulation has begun, *before* this battle takes place. Thus, it occurs sometime during the early part of the Great Tribulation.

The context in Ezekiel describes the time of the invasion as a period of relative peace for Israel (Ezekiel 38:8, 11, 14). This fits with what we know of the first half of Daniel's seventieth week.

At this time, Israel is in some sort of covenant relationship with the final Antichrist and, therefore, will supposedly be protected from any attack. This period of peace will eventually be broken at the midpoint of the seventieth week of Daniel, when the Antichrist becomes a world ruler, and the Great Tribulation, the time of Jacob's trouble, begins with its persecution of the nation of Israel.

However, at the beginning of this seven-year period, the situation will be peaceful—like the conditions when this Ezekiel invasion takes place.

OPTION 5: IT OCCURS IN THE MIDDLE, OR NEAR THE MIDDLE, OF THE FINAL SEVEN-YEAR PERIOD

This particular view believes that this invasion will take place around the middle of the final seven-year period, possibly as early as a year before. This view often identifies Ezekiel 38 and 39 with an invasion of the king of the north in Daniel 11:40. We will further explain this viewpoint as we look at the skirmish with the king of the North and the king of the South (Event 26).

Like the previous option, the fact that Israel is "living securely" (Ezekiel 38:8) is said to be the result of the false peace brought by the Antichrist during the first half of the Great Tribulation.

Thus, for three-and-a-half years, this final Gentile world ruler will encourage the Jews to return to the Holy Land. However, he will break his agreement with them and attack them with the goal of total annihilation.

Consequently, Israel will enjoy a period of peace in the Tribulation. It is during the first half of the Tribulation, toward its end, where the advocates of this view place the fulfillment of this prophecy.

OPTION 6. THIS INVASION IS THE BATTLE OF ARMAGEDDON

Many Bible teachers believe that the Gog and Magog event of Ezekiel 38, 39 is synonymous with what the Book of Revelation calls the Campaign of Armageddon (Revelation 16:16).

Since Armageddon is a huge invasion of Israel around the time of the Second Coming of Christ, and the invasion of Israel described in Ezekiel 38 and 39 is said to be in the "latter years" (Ezekiel 38:8) and "in the last days" (Ezekiel 38:16), it is claimed that they must be the same event.

OPTION 7. THE EVENTS OCCUR AT TWO DIFFERENT TIMES: CHAPTER 38 OCCURS AT THE MIDDLE OF THE TRIBULATION, CHAPTER 39 OCCURS AT THE END OF THE TRIBULATION

There are those who believe that the events of Ezekiel chapter 39 do not necessarily happen immediately following Ezekiel 38. Thus, it is contended that Ezekiel 38 takes place at the middle of the tribulation period, while Ezekiel 39 occurs some three and one-half years later at the end of this period. In this view, Ezekiel 39 is usually associated with the campaign of Armageddon.

OPTION 8. THE CONFLICT OCCURS AFTER THE SECOND COMING OF CHRIST BUT BEFORE THE MILLENNIUM

There is also the view that the invasion occurs after the Second Coming of Christ, during the interlude, or transitional time, between the Great Tribulation and the start of the Millennium. According to this perspective, since Israel will be dwelling in peace it assumes millennial-type conditions upon the earth.

OPTION 9. THE EVENTS TAKE PLACE AT THE BEGINNING OF THE MILLENNIUM

There is also the position that this event happens at the beginning of the Millennium, when Israel is living in peace with the coming of the Messiah.

OPTION 10. THESE EVENTS OCCUR AT THE END OF THE MILLENNIUM

There are those which believe that the invasion of Ezekiel 38 and 39 will occur at the end of the Millennium. Revelation 20:7–9 speaks of a conflict at the end of the thousand-year period when Satan is released. Revelation 20:8 speaks of Satan coming out to deceive the nations, which are in the four corners of the earth to gather them together for the final war against the Lord. As we find in Ezekiel 38,39, the terms Gog and Magog are also used in Revelation 20 to describe what takes place.

What is the best solution?

As we have noted, these issues are complex. To further complicate matters, this invasion is often linked to Daniel 11:40 when the Bible speaks of a skirmish between the king of the North and the king of the South. As we also mentioned, some link it instead to Armageddon (Revelation 16:16). There is also the view that all three passages are speaking of the same battle!

In our view, the best solution seems to be that the invasion will take place either shortly before the beginning of the seventieth week of Daniel, or during the early part of this last seven-year period.

Having said this, we recognize that these are certainly not the only possible answers to this complex problem. Therefore, we hold our conclusion with tentativeness as well as with humility. As we mentioned, we eventually hope to do a complete book on the subject where we can look into each of these positions in great detail.

THE ANCIENT NAMES OF THE PLAYERS

There are, however, many things that we do know about this coming invasion. We do know that Ezekiel is told that, in the "last days," a coalition of nations will form who will invade Israel. These nations are listed as follows:

The word of the Lord came to me: "Son of man, set your face against Gog, of the land of Magog, the chief prince of Meshek and Tubal; prophesy against him . . . Persia, Cush and Put will be with them, all with shields and helmets, also Gomer with all its troops, and Beth Togarmah from the far north with all its troops—the many nations with you (Ezekiel 38:1,5 NIV).

THE IDENTITY OF THESE NATIONS

The precise identity of these nations is also a matter of debate. Generally speaking, we can make the following identifications:

Ancient Name	Modern Equivalent
Rosh	Russia (or Chief)
Magog	Central Asia
Meshech and Tubal	Turkey (also southern Russia and Iran)
Persia	Iran
Cush	Northern Sudan, Ethiopia
Put	Libya
Gomer	Turkey (Armenia)
Beth-togarmah	Turkey
Many peoples	Other Islamic nations (possibly Iraq)

As with many other issues associated with this invasion, there are differences of opinion as to the precise identity of these nations. Yet, generally speaking, these seem to be the ones who will participate in this coming event.

THE SITUATION IN ISRAEL AT THE TIME OF EZEKIEL 38,39

At this time, Israel will dwell in relative security. Scripture explains their situation in this manner:

> Its people were brought out from the peoples, and all of them will be living securely (Ezekiel 38:8 NET).

The New Living Translation puts it this way:

> A long time from now you will be called into action. In the distant future you will swoop down on the land of Israel, which will be enjoying peace after recovering from war and after its people have returned from many lands to the mountains of Israel (Ezekiel 38:8 NLT).

The point is that the invasion will take place when Israel is not expecting it.

THE LORD DESTROYS THE INVADERS

Scripture records the result of the invasion:

> "Son of man, prophesy against Gog and say: 'This is what the Sovereign Lord says: I am against you, Gog, chief prince of Meshek and Tubal. I will turn you around and drag you along. I will bring you from the far north and send you against the mountains of Israel. Then I will strike your bow from your left hand and make your arrows drop from your right hand. On the mountains of Israel you will fall, you and all your troops and the nations with you. I will give you as food to all kinds of carrion birds and to the wild animals (Ezekiel 39:1-4 NIV).

The Bible emphasizes that everyone involved in this invasion from these nations will be killed.

ISRAEL WILL THEN RECOGNIZE THAT THE LORD IS INDEED GOD

The result? The nations, along with the people of Israel, will recognize that the Lord, the God of the Bible, is indeed the Lord of all! In fact, the Lord says the following:

> I will display my glory among the nations, and all the nations will see the punishment I inflict and the hand I lay on them. From that day forward the people of Israel will know that I am the Lord their God (Ezekiel 39:21,22 NIV).

To sum up, the Bible speaks of an end time invasion of Israel from seven or eight nations. This invasion will bring their armies inside the borders of the Promised Land. When this happens, the Lord will supernaturally destroy the entire invading army. This will cause all the nations, including Israel, to recognize that the Lord is God. This invasion is one of the major events of the end times.

However, exactly as to when this invasion will take place in the future is debated. As we observed, there are no less than ten different views as to the timing of this coming event.

The Amazing Scene in Heaven
(Revelation 4 and 5)

Before the events of Revelation 6-19 take place upon the earth, Scripture speaks of an event that will occur in heaven. We cannot overestimate the importance of it because this event sets the stage for all that follows.

Indeed, the fact that the Lord pulls back the curtain and gives us a glimpse of what takes place in the unseen realm ought to cause us to pay very close attention.

THE HEAVENLY SCENE

After the letters of Jesus to the seven churches in Asia, recorded in Revelation 2 and 3, the scene switches to heaven where John is supernaturally brought into the presence of the Lord:

> After this I looked, and behold, a door standing open in heaven! And the first voice, which I had heard speaking to me like a trumpet, said, "Come up here, and I will show you what must take place after this" (Revelation 4:1 ESV).

This begins the revelation of future events that are yet to take place upon the earth. As a background to these "things to come," we receive a glimpse of what takes place in heaven that will set the stage for these "last days" events.

THE HEAVENLY THRONE ROOM

Amazingly, John is brought into the actual presence of the Lord:

> And instantly I was in the Spirit, and I saw a throne in heaven and someone sitting on it. The one sitting on the throne was as brilliant as gemstones—like jasper and carnelian. And the glow of an emerald circled his throne like a rainbow (Revelation 4:2,3 NLT).

What a wonderful privilege for John! Isaiah the prophet had a similar honor:

> It was in the year King Uzziah died that I saw the Lord. He was sitting on a lofty throne, and the train of his robe filled the Temple. Attending him were mighty seraphim, each having six wings. With two wings they covered their faces, with two they covered their feet, and with two they flew. They were calling out to each other, "Holy, holy, holy is the Lord of Heaven's Armies! The whole earth is filled with his glory!" Their voices shook the Temple to its foundations, and the entire building was filled with smoke (Isaiah 6:1-4 NLT).

From the experiences of John and Isaiah, we receive a glimpse of the throne of the Lord as well as some of the supernatural beings who are in attendance.

THE TWENTY-FOUR ELDERS

John also saw twenty-four elders around the throne:

> Twenty-four thrones surrounded him, and twenty-four elders sat on them. They were all clothed in white and had gold crowns on their heads (Revelation 4:4 NLT).

As to their identity, we have looked into this question in our book *Angels*. We concluded that there is not enough evidence to determine whether they represent redeemed humans or some type of supernaturally created beings.

THE FOUR LIVING BEINGS

We also discover that in heaven there are four living beings who constantly give praise to the Lord:

> In the center and around the throne were four living beings, each covered with eyes, front and back. The first of these living beings was like a lion; the second was like an ox; the third had a human face; and the fourth was like an eagle in flight. Each of these living beings had six wings, and their wings were covered all over with eyes, inside and out. Day after day and night after night they keep on saying, "Holy, holy, holy is the Lord God, the Almighty—the one who always was, who is, and who is still to come" (Revelation 4:7-9 NLT).

The description of these four living beings has generated much discussion. We also look into their identity in our book on *Angels*. Basically, we do not know enough about them to make many specific conclusions, either.

What we do discover is that they are constantly acknowledging that the Lord is "still to come." In other words, there will come a time when Jesus Christ will return to the earth. Of course, the Book of Revelation chronicles the events leading up to His return, as well as beyond.

THE SCROLL AND THE LAMB

With this heavenly background, we are then introduced to a seven-sealed scroll:

> Then I saw a scroll in the right hand of the one who was sitting on the throne. There was writing on the inside and the outside of the scroll, and it was sealed with seven seals (Revelation 5:1-2 NLT).

At the outset, there was no creature, whether in heaven or upon the earth, that was worthy to break the seals and to open the scroll. However, there was One who did step forward, who was worthy to open the scroll:

> Then I saw a Lamb that looked as if it had been slaughtered . . . He stepped forward and took the scroll from the right hand of the one sitting on the throne (Revelation 5:6,7 NLT).

The Lamb of God is God the Son, the Lord Jesus! He will break the seals and open the scroll.

WHAT IS THE SEVEN-SEALED SCROLL? WHAT IS ITS SIGNIFICANCE?

Neither the identity of the scroll or its significance is explained to us. Consequently, there are a number of different views as to what it is, as well as what it means. They include the following four popular options:

OPTION 1: AN ANCIENT ROMAN WILL

Those who read, or heard the Book of Revelation being read out loud, would immediately identify this scroll with an ancient Roman will or "testament." These documents were sealed with six seals, each of which bore the name of the sealer. Only the sealer could open the document.

This fact has led some commentators to conclude that the scroll was God's testament concerning the promises of the inheritance of believers to His future kingdom.

OPTION 2: THE PROGRESSIVE UNFOLDING OF HISTORY

Another view sees the scroll containing the progressive unfolding of the history of the world that is contained in the Book of Revelation. As each successive seal is opened, further contents of the book are revealed.

OPTION 3: THE TITLE DEED OF ALL CREATION

The is the connection of the scroll with a "title-deed" (Jeremiah 32:10–14). Therefore, this seven-sealed scroll is the "title-deed" to creation that was forfeited by sin in Genesis. Jesus Christ has won the authority to reclaim the earth and open the scroll by His death on the cross for the sins of the world.

OPTION 4: IT IS LIKE EZEKIEL'S OR ISAIAH'S SCROLL

A fourth view sees this as similar to Ezekiel's scroll which contain "words of lament, mourning and woe" (Ezekiel 2:9–10). In other words, the contents depict the future punishments the world is about to receive.

In Isaiah 29:11, a sealed scroll is compared to the inability of the people of Israel to understand the divine message that the Isaiah is revealing:

> To you this entire prophetic revelation is like words in a sealed scroll. When they hand it to one who can read and say, "Read this," he responds, "I can't, because it is sealed." Or when they hand the scroll to one who can't read and say, "Read this," he says, "I can't read." (Isaiah 29:11 NET).

Whatever the exact meaning, it seems that the contents of the scroll cannot be revealed until the seals are broken. Therefore, the seals are hiding the contents of the scroll, God's revelation, until the seals are broken.

This heavenly scene sets the stage for all that follows. In fact, the entire panorama of the Book of Revelation is introduced with this breath-taking glimpse of heaven.

Consequently, as we begin to examine these future events that Scripture records for us, we should keep in mind this awesome background. Indeed, this should cause us to study these truths with humility as well as thankfulness to the Lord.

Therefore, it is important that all of us read these two chapters to remind ourselves of the majestic, holy, and wonderful Lord whom we serve and adore.

The Seal Judgments: The Four Horsemen of the Apocalypse (Revelation 6, 8:1)

With the opening of the sealed scroll by the Lord Jesus, the next event that we will consider is actually a series of incidents, rather than one particular occurrence that takes place at a set time. These events found in the sixth chapter of the Book of Revelation are known as the "seal judgments." We will examine each event individually.

First, there are a couple of preliminary matters which we should consider before we examine each specific event that is recorded with respect to these seal judgments.

REVELATION 6 AND THE OLIVET DISCOURSE

It has been observed by Bible students that the order of events found in this chapter is very similar to the order of the events that Jesus predicted in the Olivet Discourse—His Sermon on the Mount of Olives (Matthew 24, Luke 21).

In fact, these particular passages are key to understanding the outline of this part of the Book of Revelation. The events that the Lord spoke about include the appearance of many antichrists, continuing war, famine, death, the martyrdom of believers, and signs that occur upon the earth as well as in heaven. Each of these are found in the "seal judgments."

In fact, in Matthew 24:15, Jesus spoke of a particular sign of the end which occurs in the middle of the seventieth week of Daniel—the abomination of desolation:

> So when you see standing in the holy place 'the abomination that causes desolation,' spoken of through the prophet Daniel—let the reader understand (Matthew 24:15 NIV).

THE FIRST THREE AND ONE-HALF YEARS ARE THE BEGINNING OF BIRTH PAINS

Consequently, the events that He described *before* the midpoint of this final seven-year period (Matthew 24:4-14) are what is found in these first six seals. They will most likely occur in the first half of the final seven years before the coming of Christ. Jesus referred to this three and one-half year period as the "beginning of birth pains." The Lord said:

> All these are the beginning of birth pains (Matthew 24:8 NIV).

Hence, in Revelation chapter six, we find the earth beginning to experience these judgments from the Lord.

THE FIRST SEAL: THE RIDER ON THE WHITE HORSE

The message from the first seal concerns a rider on a white horse. It reads as follows:

> I watched as the Lamb opened the first of the seven seals. Then I heard one of the four living creatures say in a voice like thunder, "Come!" I looked, and there before me was a white horse! Its rider held a bow, and he was given a crown, and he rode out as a conqueror bent on conquest (Revelation 6:1-2 NIV).

The "Lamb" who opens these seals is the risen Christ. In other words, the judgments which are coming upon the earth are His doing.

IS THE RIDER CHRIST OR ANTICHRIST?

There is disagreement as to the identity of this "rider." Some see this as a reference to the conquering Christ. This would be consistent with the "overcomer" theme of the Book of Revelation. Indeed, we find that the Lord Jesus returns to the earth while riding upon a "white horse" (Revelation 19).

However, since we find evil associated with all of the other riders, this first rider is best understood as the beast—the final Antichrist. He will be the evil ruler of the Great Tribulation period.

We will also discover that this man is a wicked parody of Jesus. In other words, he will mimic Christ in a number of evil ways. In addition, though this beast will establish a worldwide rule by force, he will first appear on the stage of history as a "man of peace."

Jesus warned of false Christs that would appear:

> Watch out that no one misleads you. For many will come in my name, saying, 'I am the Christ,' and they will mislead many (Matthew 24:4,5 NET).

In this instance, this rider on the white horse will be the ultimate pretender. Indeed, he will be a "man of peace" who turns out to be a horrible monster.

THE SECOND SEAL: WAR BREAKS OUT UPON THE EARTH

The opening of the second seal reveals a red horse. What follows next is war upon the earth. The Bible says:

> When the Lamb opened the second seal, I heard the second living creature say, "Come!" Then another horse came out, a fiery red one. Its rider was given power to take peace from the earth and to make people kill each other. To him was given a large sword (Revelation 6:3-4 NIV).

When peace is removed from the earth, Scripture says that the people of the world will turn upon one another. The symbol of the huge sword likely represents a tremendous loss of life.

Again, we find that Jesus warned that this would happen:

> You will hear of wars and rumors of wars. Make sure that you are not alarmed, for this must happen, but the end is still to come. For nation will rise up in arms against nation, and kingdom against kingdom (Matthew 24:6,7 NET).

THE THIRD SEAL: FAMINE AND ITS AFTERMATH

The next horse is black. This horse is described as follows:

> When the Lamb opened the third seal, I heard the third living creature say, "Come!" I looked, and there before me was a black horse! Its rider was holding a pair of scales in his hand. Then I heard what sounded like a voice among the four living creatures, saying, "Two pounds of wheat for a day's wages, and six pounds of barley for a day's wages, and do not damage the oil and the wine!" (Revelation 6:5-6 NIV).

The scales could represent either judgment, in general, or the instrument used to weigh the terribly scarce food that will exist at this time.

Others see this representing famine and inflation. In fact, inflation has been estimated to reach 1,000 percent! The result of this judgment will be a universal famine that will come upon the inhabitants of the earth.

Once again, this will fulfill the prediction of the Lord Jesus:

> There will be famines (Matthew 24:7 NIV).

THE FOURTH SEAL: DEATH AND HADES

The fourth seal reveals a horse with a pale rider upon it. It predicts a terrible punishment upon those living on the earth. Scripture says:

When the Lamb opened the fourth seal, I heard the voice of the fourth living creature say, "Come!" I looked, and there before me was a pale horse! Its rider was named Death, and Hades was following close behind him. They were given power over a fourth of the earth to kill by sword, famine and plague, and by the wild beasts of the earth (Revelation 6:7-8 NIV).

Death is personified as a rider upon this fourth horse, with Hades following right behind. We find that these two terms are often coupled in the Book of Revelation (see 1:18, 6:8, 20:13-14).

Hades is sometimes used in the Bible to describe the place where the dead reside. Later, in Revelation, it will specifically refer to the place where the unbelieving dead are kept while awaiting the "Last Judgment" (For more on the subject of Hades, see our book *What Happens One Second After We Die?*).

The ashen, or pale, color of the horse could mean a number of things. Some suggest that it pictures the putrefaction of human flesh. This would make sense considering the magnitude of the human loss of life during this global judgment, where one quarter of the population of the earth will die. Such a tremendous number of corpses will make a timely burial of the deceased impossible for those who survive. Hence, the putrefying of human flesh will occur on a grand scale.

Jesus also warned about the future pestilence that is mentioned here:

There will be great earthquakes, famines and pestilences in various places, and fearful events and great signs from heaven (Luke 21:11 NIV).

In sum, sword, famine, and pestilence summarize the second, third, and fourth seal judgments. The destruction that will be caused by "wild beasts" further emphasizes the commotion that will characterize this time period. Unfortunately, for the people of this world, it is only the beginning.

THE FIFTH SEAL: THE SOULS UNDER THE ALTAR

The fifth seal reveals that many people will be martyred for their faith in Jesus Christ:

> When he opened the fifth seal, I saw under the altar the souls of those who had been slain because of the word of God and the testimony they had maintained (Revelation 6:9 NIV).

Jesus warned that this would happen to those living at this time:

> Then you will be handed over to be persecuted and put to death, and you will be hated by all nations because of me (Matthew 24:9 NIV).

THE SIXTH SEAL: THE COSMIC UPHEAVAL

The next seal reveals momentous events upon the earth as well as in the sky:

> I watched as he opened the sixth seal. There was a great earthquake. The sun turned black like sackcloth made of goat hair, the whole moon turned blood red, and the stars in the sky fell to earth, as figs drop from a fig tree when shaken by a strong wind. The heavens receded like a scroll being rolled up, and every mountain and island was removed from its place (Revelation 6:12-14 NIV).

This will cause panic to grip the people of the earth. Indeed, the inhabitants will realize that the wrath of God is being poured out upon this godless world:

> Then the kings of the earth, the princes, the generals, the rich, the mighty, and everyone else, both slave and free, hid in caves and among the rocks of the mountains. They called to the mountains and the rocks, "Fall on us and hide us from the face of him who sits on the throne and from the wrath

of the Lamb! For the great day of their wrath has come, and who can withstand it?" (Revelation 6:15-17 NIV).

Jesus warned that such a time would come:

> There will be signs in the sun, moon and stars. On the earth, nations will be in anguish and perplexity at the roaring and tossing of the sea. People will faint from terror, apprehensive of what is coming on the world, for the heavenly bodies will be shaken (Luke 21:25, 26 NIV).

THE SEVENTH SEAL: SILENCE IN HEAVEN

After an interlude, we have the description of the seventh seal:

> When he opened the seventh seal, there was silence in heaven for about half an hour. And I saw the seven angels who stand before God, and seven trumpets were given to them (Revelation 8:1,2 NET).

The seventh seal is different than the first six seals in that it has no content of its own. Instead, it introduces us to the next group of judgments—the trumpets.

This completes the opening of the seven-sealed document and what seems to be the first three and a half years of the seven-year Great Tribulation period. Soon, the trumpet judgments would begin.

The Rise of the Final Antichrist (1 John 2:18)

The Bible speaks of an evil personage who will come on the scene of history at the time of the end. This individual will be like no one else who has ever lived. He will be the final Gentile world ruler. He is known in Scripture by many names, with the most popular being the "Beast," the "Man of Sin," and the "Antichrist."

Scripture tells us a number of things about the events in the life of this coming man of sin—the final Antichrist. Though we cannot be absolutely certain about the exact chronology of these events, we are able to list the following lowlights as we continue our look at the "things to come."

1. HE WILL APPEAR AT THE TIME OF THE END

Scripture is clear that this final Antichrist will not appear on the stage of history until the time of the end. The Lord said the following to the prophet Daniel in a vision relating to the final Antichrist:

> As Gabriel approached the place where I was standing, I became so terrified that I fell with my face to the ground. "Son of man," he said, "you must understand that the events you have seen in your vision relate to the time of the end" (Daniel 8:17 NLT).

Indeed, his coming signals the time of the end. He cannot appear before these "last days" since his coming sets the stage for the soon return of Jesus Christ to the earth. Therefore, it is clear that the final Antichrist has not yet publicly arrived on the scene.

2. HIS ARRIVAL WILL SIGNAL THE BEGINNING OF THE PROPHETIC PERIOD, THE DAY OF THE LORD

The Bible says that Antichrist's coming will commence a prophetic period known as the "day of the Lord." Paul wrote about this time to the church at Thessalonica. He said:

> And now, brothers and sisters, let us tell you about the coming again of our Lord Jesus Christ and how we will be gathered together to meet him. Please don't be so easily shaken and troubled by those who say that the day of the Lord has already begun. Even if they claim to have had a vision, a revelation, or a letter supposedly from us, don't believe them. Don't be fooled by what they say. For that day will not come until there is a great rebellion against God and the man of lawlessness is revealed—the one who brings destruction (2 Thessalonians 2:1-3 NLT).

This period cannot begin until the final Antichrist arrives on the scene.

3. HE IS PRESENTLY BEING RESTRAINED BY SOMEONE OR SOMETHING

We know that someone or something is presently restraining the appearance of this final Antichrist. Paul wrote the following to the Thessalonians:

> And you know what is holding him back, for he can be revealed only when his time comes (2 Thessalonians 2:6 NLT).

The pre-tribulation rapture view holds that the Lord will remove the true believers out of the world before the Great Tribulation period.

According to this position, immediately following the rapture of the church, the final Antichrist will be revealed. Until that time, his identity will remain unknown to the world.

The reason he cannot be revealed before this time is because the Holy Spirit of God, through the believers living upon the earth, is presently restraining this coming "man of sin." Once the believers are removed through the rapture, this evil personage can then be revealed.

Other views of the rapture of the church (the mid-tribulation, the pre-wrath, and post-tribulation view) believe the restrainer of Antichrist consists of something else. However, all agree on this point: the final Antichrist is presently being restrained.

4. HE WILL APPEAR AS AN INCONSPICUOUS FIGURE

Antichrist appears on the scene of world history as an inconspicuous figure. This is explained for us in the Book of Daniel. We read of his rise from obscurity:

> After that, in my vision at night I looked, and there before me was a fourth beast—terrifying and frightening and very powerful. It had large iron teeth; it crushed and devoured its victims and trampled underfoot whatever was left. It was different from all the former beasts, and it had ten horns. "While I was thinking about the horns, there before me was another horn, a little one, which came up among them; and three of the first horns were uprooted before it. This horn had eyes like the eyes of a human being and a mouth that spoke boastfully" (Daniel 7:7-8 NIV).

He is called a "little horn." This seems to indicate that his rise is from relative obscurity. Therefore, he will not be someone who has an immediate high profile.

5. HE WILL APPEAR AS A MAN OF PEACE

He starts out upon a career of conquest by peaceful means. As we mentioned, when we looked at the judgment of the "seven seals," the Book of Revelation introduces us to the four horsemen of the apocalypse. Scripture says:

> I watched as the Lamb opened the first of the seven seals. Then I heard one of the four living creatures say in a voice like thunder, "Come!" I looked, and there before me was a white horse! Its rider held a bow, and he was given a crown, and he rode out as a conqueror bent on conquest (Revelation 6:1–2 NIV).

The final Antichrist is portrayed here as the rider on a white horse. He will begin his career by peaceful means as a "conqueror bent on conquest."

6. HE WILL RECEIVE A FATAL HEAD WOUND

This seems to be *the* significant event in the life of the coming Antichrist. Scripture tells us that his personality changes after he receives this fatal wound to the head. The Bible says:

> One of its heads seemed to have a mortal wound, but its mortal wound was healed, and the whole earth marveled as they followed the beast (Revelation 13:3 ESV).

Whether or not he actually dies, it certainly appears that way to everyone upon the earth.

7. HE WILL DESCEND INTO THE ABYSS

After this head wound occurs, this personage descends into the abyss—the bottomless pit. The Book of Revelation says:

> And when they [the two witnesses] have finished their testimony, the beast that rises from the bottomless pit will make

war on them and conquer them and kill them (Revelation 11:7 ESV).

The abyss is the bottomless pit—the prison house of evil spirits. The beast becomes a different person after he goes down into the abyss, and then returns.

8. HE IS RAISED BACK TO LIFE: THE WORLD IS AMAZED

Something happens to this political leader at this point, he is raised back to life. This event is described as follows:

> One of the beast's heads appeared to have been killed, but the lethal wound had been healed. And the whole world followed the beast in amazement. . . He exercised all the ruling authority of the first beast on his behalf, and made the earth and those who inhabit it worship the first beast, the one whose lethal wound had been healed. . . and, by the signs he was permitted to perform on behalf of the beast, he deceived those who live on the earth. He told those who live on the earth to make an image to the beast who had been wounded by the sword, but still lived (Revelation 13:3,12,14 NET).

This causes the people of the world to be astonished. The Word of God puts it this way:

> The beast that you saw was, and is not, and is about to rise from the bottomless pit and go to destruction. And the dwellers on earth whose names have not been written in the book of life from the foundation of the world will marvel to see the beast, because it was and is not and is to come (Revelation 17:8 ESV).

This beast seemingly rises from the dead.

9. HE BECOMES THE BEAST, A MAN CONTROLLED BY SATAN

This man goes from a world leader in politics, to a worldwide dictator. He is now, officially, the beast—a satanically controlled individual. The Bible says:

> Now the beast that I saw was like a leopard, but its feet were like a bear's, and its mouth was like a lion's mouth. The dragon gave the beast his power, his throne, and great authority to rule. One of the beast's heads appeared to have been killed, but the lethal wound had been healed. And the whole world followed the beast in amazement; they worshiped the dragon because he had given ruling authority to the beast, and they worshiped the beast too, saying: "Who is like the beast?" and "Who is able to make war against him?" The beast was given a mouth speaking proud words and blasphemies, and he was permitted to exercise ruling authority for forty-two months (Revelation 13:2-5 NET).

There is an entire change of character of this personage.

10. HE RULES POLITICALLY AND CURSES THE LIVING GOD

The political rule of the entire world begins. The Bible says the following will happen:

> They worshiped the dragon for giving the beast such power, and they also worshiped the beast. "Who is as great as the beast?" they exclaimed. "Who is able to fight against him?" Then the beast was allowed to speak great blasphemies against God. And he was given authority to do whatever he wanted for forty-two months. And he spoke terrible words of blasphemy against God, slandering his name and his dwelling—that is, those who dwell in heaven. And the beast was allowed to wage war against God's holy people and to conquer them. And he was given authority to rule over every tribe and people and language and nation. And all the people who belong to this world worshiped the beast. They are the ones whose names were not written in the Book of Life before the world was made—the Book that belongs to the Lamb who was slaughtered (Revelation 13:4-8 NLT).

As a worldwide ruler, the beast feels free to curse the God of Scripture.

The Book of Daniel talks about this personage who will speak boastfully. We read:

> While I was thinking about the horns, there before me was another horn, a little one, which came up among them; and three of the first horns were uprooted before it. This horn had eyes like the eyes of a human being and a mouth that spoke boastfully (Daniel 7:8 NIV).

Thus, his ability to speak boastfully is emphasized in both testaments.

11. HE WILL ATTEMPT TO MAKE CHANGES IN THE CALENDAR

He will also attempt to make changes in the calendar that have been established by the law:

> He will speak words against the Most High. He will harass the holy ones of the Most High continually. His intention will be to change times established by law (Daniel 7:25 NET).

This could refer to the calendar itself, or it may be a specific reference to the changing of "holy days." In other words, he may change the way the calendar is dated as A.D. and B.C., refuse to recognize Easter and Christmas, etc. In sum, there will be no acknowledgement of Jesus Christ as long as he is ruling.

Interestingly, there was an unsuccessful attempt during the time of the French Revolution to replace the Christian (Gregorian) calendar with a Revolutionary calendar. It seems the final Antichrist will do something similar.

This briefly sums up the career of the final Antichrist. As we will observe when we examine other future events, this evil personage will play a large part in many of them.

For a thorough look at this coming "man of sin" see our book *The Final Antichrist: The Coming Caesar*.

The Covenant between the Final Antichrist and the Jews: The Seventieth Week of Daniel Begins (Daniel 9:27)

This is one of the most important events in all of Scripture. In fact, it will start the clock ticking for the final seven-year period of our present age. At the end of the seven years, Jesus Christ will return to the earth.

THE ANTICHRIST WILL MAKE A PEACE TREATY WITH ISRAEL

The final Antichrist makes, or confirms, a peace treaty with the Jews, a covenant of peace. We have already referred to this in our discussion of preliminary matters. Here we will examine this agreement, or covenant, in more detail. Again, Daniel 9:27 is the key verse:

> He will make a treaty with the people for a period of one set of seven (Daniel 9:27 NLT).

There is some question as to the meaning of the Hebrew word in this verse translated as "confirm." It could mean "force upon." In other words, this "man of sin" will compel Israel to make this agreement.

The phrase "one set of seven" refers to a period of seven years. It constitutes a seven-year agreement that involves the nation of Israel.

This "man of lawlessness" will do all of this in his own name, or authority. Jesus said of him:

> I have come in my Father's name, and you do not receive
> me. If another comes in his own name, you will receive him
> (John 5:43 ESV).

Because of this "peace treaty," Antichrist will be welcomed by the Jews. Israel, which has rejected Jesus as their Messiah, will receive this "man of sin."

This particular peace treaty will begin the seventieth week of Daniel— the last seven years in this present age before Jesus Christ returns. Therefore, this is a very significant event.

THIS TREATY WILL INVOLVE JERUSALEM AND THE TEMPLE MOUNT

This treaty will seemingly allow the Jews to take possession of the area of the Temple Mount—the place where the First and Second Temple stood. We read about the measuring of the Temple in the Book of Revelation. It says.

> Then I was given a measuring rod like a staff, and I was
> told, "Rise and measure the temple of God and the altar
> and those who worship there, but do not measure the court
> outside the temple; leave that out, for it is given over to the
> nations, and they will trample the holy city for forty-two
> months. And I will grant authority to my two witnesses,
> and they will prophesy for 1,260 days, clothed in sackcloth"
> (Revelation 11:1–3 ESV).

The fact that the temple is measured assumes that it exists at that time. We are not told what Antichrist receives in return for making this deal with the nation.

To sum up, this agreement is central to the events that will take place at the time of the end.

The Abomination of Desolation
the Beginning of the Great Tribulation
(Matthew 24:15)

One of the major coming events, as far as Scripture is concerned, is known as the "abomination of desolation," or the "abomination that causes desolation." This will take place at the midpoint of the final seven-year period—the seventieth week of Daniel.

The "peace agreement," made between the Jews and the Antichrist, will also be broken in the midst of this final seven-year period. The Bible explains it this way:

> He will confirm a covenant with many for one 'seven.' In the middle of the 'seven' he will put an end to sacrifice and offering. And at the temple he will set up an abomination that causes desolation, until the end that is decreed is poured out on him (Daniel 9:27 NIV).

Antichrist will put an end to the sacrifices being offered in the Temple. He will then turn upon the nation which embraced him.

Paul wrote about what will occur when the people think they are at peace:

> Now, brothers and sisters, about times and dates we do not need to write to you, for you know very well that the day of

the Lord will come like a thief in the night. While people are saying, "Peace and safety," destruction will come on them suddenly, as labor pains on a pregnant woman, and they will not escape (1 Thessalonians 5:1-3 NIV).

There will be no safety for them. In fact, when they think they have peace then destruction will suddenly come upon them.

ANTICHRIST DESECRATES THE TEMPLE IN JERUSALEM

The holiest spot on earth for the Jews is the Temple Mount in Jerusalem. It was the site of the First and Second Temple and will also be the site of the Third Temple.

This Third Temple now becomes a place of desecration. The "man of sin," who is the unholiest of all the people on the earth, comes to the most Holy Place. Indeed, in five different places in Scripture we are told of this horrific event (Daniel 9:27, Daniel 12:11, Matthew 24:15, 2 Thessalonians 2:1-4, Revelation 11:2).

This beast, Antichrist, will claim Deity for himself. Paul wrote:

He will exalt himself and defy every god there is and tear down every object of adoration and worship. He will position himself in the temple of God, claiming that he himself is God (2 Thessalonians 2:4 NLT).

He defies the living God and makes outrageous claims. Included is the claim to Deity. This beast offers himself to the world as a god in the place of Jesus Christ—the true and living God. He is truly an "anti" Christ.

Scripture says that once this event takes place, people can start marking time. Indeed, it will be 1,290 days until the return of the Lord:

From the time the daily sacrifice is abolished and the abomination of desolation is set up, there will be 1,290 days.

Happy is the one who waits for and reaches 1,335 days (Daniel 12:11 CSB)

Consequently, this "abomination that causes desolation" is a landmark event of the time of the end. Indeed, it signifies the beginning of the Great Tribulation Period.

For more on the events surrounding this future Temple, see our books *The Jews, Jerusalem and the Coming Temple* as well as *25 Signs We Are Near the End.*

The Sealing of 144,000
(Revelation 7:14)

After the recording of judgment of the first six seals (Revelation 6), there is an interlude before the seventh seal is broken (Revelation 8). During this interlude, we are introduced to a special group of individuals—the 144,000. This group of people will evangelize the world with the message of Christ. The Bible describes them as follows:

> Then I saw another angel rising up from the east, who had the seal of the living God. He cried out in a loud voice to the four angels who were allowed to harm the earth and the sea: "Don't harm the earth or the sea or the trees until we seal the servants of our God on their foreheads." And I heard the number of the sealed: 144,000 sealed from every tribe of the Israelites: 12,000 sealed from the tribe of Judah, 12,000 from the tribe of Reuben, 12,000 from the tribe of Gad, 12,000 from the tribe of Asher, 12,000 from the tribe of Naphtali, 12,000 from the tribe of Manasseh, 12,000 from the tribe of Simeon, 12,000 from the tribe of Levi, 12,000 from the tribe of Issachar, 12,000 from the tribe of Zebulun, 12,000 from the tribe of Joseph, 12,000 sealed from the tribe of Benjamin (Revelation 7:2-8 CSB).

There are a number of questions that arise with respect to the 144,000.

IS THIS PASSAGE LITERAL OR SYMBOLIC?

The first question that needs to be answered concerns whether this passage is to be interpreted in a literal manner or symbolically. The specific references to Israel, and the names of their 12 tribes, strongly suggests that the nation of Israel is in view. However, there are those who believe that this passage is to be interpreted symbolically.

DOES IT REPRESENT SPIRITUAL ISRAEL?

Many interpreters believe the 144,000 are members of "spiritual Israel"— a title of theirs for the church. They assume that the number is symbolic of all God's servants in the Great Tribulation.

RESPONSE TO THE SYMBOLIC VIEWPOINT

The case for symbolism in this passage is not very convincing. Indeed, the main problem with this view is an attempt to make the 144,000 into a group representative of the church. However, there is seemingly no possible numerical connection to the church that exists. Indeed, there is no basis to understand the simple statement of fact in Revelation 7:4 as a figure of speech.

UNCONVERTED JEWS

There is also the perspective that interprets these people as literal Jews who are not converted. These orthodox Jews will resist the seduction of the Antichrist as well as be supernaturally kept from dying during the Great Tribulation. Eventually they will accept Jesus Christ as their Savior when He returns at the Second Coming, and they will populate the millennial kingdom.

The problem with this view is that these witnesses—the 144,000— appear to be believers in Jesus Christ.

THE LITERAL VIEW: 144,000 CONVERTED JEWS

The best view is the literal view. The fact that this is a definite number of people can be seen in the very next verse with the contrast to the indefinite number of people:

> After this I looked, and behold, a great multitude that no one could number, from every nation, from all tribes and peoples and languages, standing before the throne and before the Lamb, clothed in white robes, with palm branches in their hands (Revelation 7:9 ESV).

Therefore, the author had no problem speaking of an indefinite number of people when the situation warranted it. The fact that the 144,000 are specifically mentioned, as opposed to the indefinite number of the great multitude, is another reason to assume that we are talking about a literal group of people with a defined number.

In addition, since there is no reason to understand the "great multitude" as a symbolic group, it follows that the 144,000 should likewise not be interpreted symbolically.

In fact, if this number is interpreted symbolically, then no number in the entire book of Revelation can be taken literally.

FURTHER EXPLANATION OF THE 144,000

The view that these are actual Israelites, who believe in Jesus, is further illustrated later in the Book of Revelation:

> Then I looked, and here was the Lamb standing on Mount Zion, and with him were one hundred and forty-four thousand, who had his name and his Father's name written on their foreheads. I also heard a sound coming out of heaven like the sound of many waters and like the sound of loud thunder. Now the sound I heard was like that made by harpists playing their harps, and they were singing a new song

before the throne and before the four living creatures and the elders. No one was able to learn the song except the one hundred and forty-four thousand who had been redeemed from the earth. These are the ones who have not defiled themselves with women, for they are virgins. These are the ones who follow the Lamb wherever he goes. These were redeemed from humanity as firstfruits to God and to the Lamb, and no lie was found on their lips; they are blameless (Revelation 14:1-5 NET)

This later vision of John brings us to the time of the Second Coming of Christ. The Lord joins the 144,000 on literal Mount Zion, which is earthly Jerusalem, at the beginning of His one thousand-year reign upon the earth —the Millennium. Along with various groups of supernatural beings, the 144,000 will sing a new song to the Lord.

THEY DID NOT ENGAGE IN FALSE WORSHIP

The most likely meaning of the phrase "not being defiled with women" is that they have not engaged in the false worship that will take place during the Great Tribulation period. In other words, they did not commit spiritual adultery. In the Old Testament, we often find that the idolatry of Israel was described as spiritual adultery (Exodus 34:11-17, Hosea 1:2; 2:2).

THEY ARE THE FIRST OF MANY

Furthermore, these believers are the firstfruits of those from Israel who will have trusted Christ. Many of the descendants of Abraham, Isaac and Jacob will follow them into God's family by believing in Jesus Christ during the Great Tribulation period.

In sum, the 144,000, are exactly what they appear to be: twelve thousand Jews from each of the twelve tribes of Israel.

EVENT 13

The Trumpet Judgments
(Revelation 8, 9)

As we earlier observed, the first set of judgments recorded in the Book of Revelation are the "seven seals." They seem to cover the first half of the last seven-year period—the "seventieth week of Daniel."

The "Abomination of Desolation" spoken of Matthew 24:15, is the starting point for the second half of this seven-year period. It is during this period that we also discover that two other sets of judgments will come upon those who live on the earth at this time: the "trumpet" judgments and the "bowl" judgments.

THE TRUMPETS

The next set of judgments in the Book of Revelation are known as the "trumpet" judgments. These judgments take place after the "seal" Judgments and most likely occur in the last half of the Great Tribulation.

THERE ARE PARALLELS WITH THE EXODUS

While the seal judgments fulfill Jesus' predictions about conditions during the first half of this last seven-year period, the events associated with the trumpets strongly parallel events connected with the exodus of Israel from Egypt during the second half of this last seven-year period. In contrast to what happened during the days of Moses, however, these judgments will take place on a worldwide scale.

THE FIRST TRUMPET: DESTRUCTION UPON THE LAND

The trumpet judgments begin with the earth itself. The Bible says the following will take place:

> The first angel blew his trumpet, and hail and fire, mixed with blood, were hurled to the earth. So a third of the earth was burned up, a third of the trees were burned up, and all the green grass was burned up. (Revelation 8:7 CSB).

This first trumpet judgment consists of a number of elements that will be hurled down from the sky to the earth. The hail and fire, mixed with blood, will destroy one-third of the remaining vegetation on the earth. Of course, this will only intensify the famine that was earlier introduced during the seal judgments.

THE EXODUS PARALLEL

The first trumpet is reminiscent of the plague of hail sent by the Lord upon Egypt:

> Then the Lord said to Moses, "Stretch out your hand toward heaven and let there be hail throughout the land of Egypt— on people and animals and every plant of the field in the land of Egypt." So Moses stretched out his staff toward heaven, and the Lord sent thunder and hail. Lightning struck the land, and the Lord rained hail on the land of Egypt. The hail, with lightning flashing through it, was so severe that nothing like it had occurred in the land of Egypt since it had become a nation. Throughout the land of Egypt, the hail struck down everything in the field, both people and animals. The hail beat down every plant of the field and shattered every tree in the field (Exodus 9:22-25 CSB).

THE SECOND TRUMPET: JUDGMENT UPON THE SEA

The second trumpet judgment will cause something like a great burning mountain to be hurled into the sea. The Bible says:

The second angel sounded his trumpet, and something like a huge mountain, all ablaze, was thrown into the sea. A third of the sea turned into blood, a third of the living creatures in the sea died, and a third of the ships were destroyed (Revelation 8:8-9 CSB).

Hence, after striking the land with the blowing of the first trumpet, the Lord then turns to the sea. This will cause problems with all sea life as well as with human commerce. A great mountain that burns with fire, which possibly describes a giant meteor, will be hurled into the sea by the Lord.

The consequences are enormous. In fact, one-third of all life in the sea will perish. This huge loss of aquatic life will be so vast, it will cause the sea to turn red with blood. In addition, not only will a major food source vanish from the earth, countless ships will also be lost, along with their crews.

THE EXODUS PARALLEL

This second trumpet reminds us of the Lord turning the water into blood in Egypt:

> Moses and Aaron did just as the Lord had commanded; in the sight of Pharaoh and his officials, he raised the staff and struck the water in the Nile, and all the water in the Nile was turned to blood. The fish in the Nile died, and the river smelled so bad the Egyptians could not drink water from it. There was blood throughout the land of Egypt (Exodus 7:20-21 CSB).

THE THIRD TRUMPET: THE FRESH WATER IS POLLUTED

The next trumpet judgment concerns the pollution of the fresh waters of the earth. Scripture records what will occur as follows:

> The third angel blew his trumpet, and a great star, blazing like a torch, fell from heaven. It fell on a third of the rivers

and springs of water. The name of the star is Wormwood, and a third of the waters became wormwood. So, many of the people died from the waters, because they had been made bitter (Revelation 8:10-11 CSB).

This third trumpet judgment will cause the earth's fresh water supply to be polluted. This will be accomplished by a falling star named "Wormwood."

This judgment will ruin the taste as well as the purity of the world's most essential resource—water. The result is that many people will die because of this punishment.

THIS WILL REMIND THE PEOPLE OF THE IDENTITY OF THE REAL GOD

Interestingly, the Bible records a similar meteoric stone that was used as the pedestal of the image of the goddess Diana in the city of Ephesus. In fact, the city clerk of Ephesus referred to this when he reminded the Ephesians that their city was the temple-keeper of the great Diana, and of the image which fell down from heaven:

> The city clerk quieted the crowd and said: "Fellow Ephesians, doesn't all the world know that the city of Ephesus is the guardian of the temple of the great Artemis and of her image, which fell from heaven?" (Acts 19:35 NIV).

Among other things, it seems that this particular judgment will make it clear to the world who is God as well as who is not!

This event also parallels the Exodus account of the Lord turning the water of the Nile River into blood.

THE FOURTH TRUMPET: THE JUDGMENT UPON THE HEAVENLY BODIES

The fourth trumpet announces judgment upon the heavenly bodies. The Bible says:

The fourth angel blew his trumpet, and a third of the sun was struck, a third of the moon, and a third of the stars, so that a third of them were darkened. A third of the day was without light and also a third of the night (Revelation 8:12 CSB).

As the fourth angel blew his trumpet, John viewed the devastating damage taking place among the heavenly bodies. The result of such a cataclysmic punishment will be an unprecedented amount of darkness, both day and night. This lack of sunlight will also lead to agonizing cold for those living upon the earth.

THE EXODUS PARALLEL

This punishment will immediately remind the believers of the darkness the Lord sent to the Land of Egypt:

Then the Lord said to Moses, "Stretch out your hand toward heaven, and there will be darkness over the land of Egypt, a darkness that can be felt." So Moses stretched out his hand toward heaven, and there was thick darkness throughout the land of Egypt for three days. One person could not see another, and for three days they did not move from where they were. Yet all the Israelites had light where they lived (Exodus 10:21-23 CSB).

THE COMING THREE WOES

After these first four judgments, a soaring eagle then announces a triple "woe" which will come upon the earth:

As I watched, I heard an eagle that was flying in midair call out in a loud voice: "Woe! Woe! Woe to the inhabitants of the earth, because of the trumpet blasts about to be sounded by the other three angels!" (Revelation 8:13 NIV).

This is in anticipation of the last three trumpet judgments. The idea behind this pronouncement is that the worst judgments are still to come!

As we have observed, the first four trumpet judgments will affect the natural world. However, the last three will be directly aimed at the people living upon the earth.

THE FIFTH TRUMPET: DEMONS AFFLICT THOSE UPON THE EARTH

The fifth trumpet judgment, the first "woe," involves the world of the supernatural. The Bible says that demons will come and terribly afflict those still living upon the earth (Revelation 8:13–9:12).

THE STAR FALLING FROM HEAVEN

In this fifth judgment, a wicked angel will be allowed to release the demonic inhabitants of the bottomless pit. They are described as locusts:

> And out of the smoke locusts came down on the earth and were given power like that of scorpions of the earth (Revelation 9:2 NIV).

They seem to be the rebellious angels that Peter wrote about:

> For if God didn't spare the angels who sinned but cast them into hell and delivered them in chains of utter darkness to be kept for judgment; and if he didn't spare the ancient world, but protected Noah, a preacher of righteousness, and seven others, when he brought the flood on the world of the ungodly; and if he reduced the cities of Sodom and Gomorrah to ashes and condemned them to extinction, making them an example of what is coming to the ungodly (2 Peter 2:4-6)

PEOPLE WILL BE THE TARGET OF THESE WICKED ANGELS

As we mentioned, the first four trumpet judgments only affected the inhabitants of the earth indirectly. Now, however, these last three trumpet judgments will be directed upon the humans who have not believed in Jesus Christ:

The locusts looked like horses prepared for battle. On their heads they wore something like crowns of gold, and their faces resembled human faces. Their hair was like women's hair, and their teeth were like lions' teeth. They had breastplates like breastplates of iron, and the sound of their wings was like the thundering of many horses and chariots rushing into battle. They had tails with stingers, like scorpions, and in their tails they had power to torment people for five months (Revelation 9:7-10 NIV).

The grotesque appearance of these creatures that come down on the earth during this fifth judgment will be terrifying to the people living at this time.

THE LEADER ABADDON (APOLLYON)

The ruler, the king over this fiendish horde of demons, bore two names:

They had as king over them the angel of the Abyss, whose name in Hebrew is Abaddon and in Greek is Apollyon (that is, Destroyer) (Revelation 9:11 NIV).

As this verse explains, the Hebrew word *Abaddon* and the Greek *Apollyon* have the meaning of "destruction" or "destroyer."

THE PARALLEL WITH EXODUS

This fifth trumpet is paralleled in the Book of Exodus with the punishment that was sent upon the people from a supernatural source. In this instance, it was the Lord Himself:

At midnight the Lord struck down all the firstborn in Egypt, from the firstborn of Pharaoh, who sat on the throne, to the firstborn of the prisoner, who was in the dungeon, and the firstborn of all the livestock as well. Pharaoh and all his officials and all the Egyptians got up during the night, and there was loud wailing in Egypt, for there was not a house without someone dead (Exodus 12:29,30 NIV).

TWO WOES ARE STILL TO COME

With the sounding of the fifth trumpet, the trouble is yet to be over:

The first woe is past; two other woes are yet to come (Revelation 9:12 NIV).

This warning anticipates the remaining trumpet judgments. In fact, the worst is still to come.

EVENT 14

The Sixth Trumpet: The Two Hundred Million Man Army (Revelation 9:13-21)

Thus far we have considered the first five of the trumpet judgments. By far, the worst judgment is found in the judgment associated with the sixth trumpet.

THE SIXTH TRUMPET: THE RELEASE OF FOUR DEMONIC CREATURES

With the introduction of the sixth trumpet, John heard a voice that sounded from the altar, the place of worship in heaven:

> The sixth angel sounded his trumpet, and I heard a voice coming from the four horns of the golden altar that is before God. It said to the sixth angel who had the trumpet, "Release the four angels who are bound at the great river Euphrates." And the four angels who had been kept ready for this very hour and day and month and year were released to kill a third of mankind (Revelation 9:13-15 NIV).

An unidentified voice commands this sixth angel to release four destructive angels who have been bound at the Euphrates River. Their release will cause a third of the human race to be killed!

THE TWO HUNDRED MILLION MAN ARMY

We then read of a huge army of soldiers on horseback:

The number of soldiers on horseback was two hundred million; I heard their number (Revelation 9:16 NET).

Two hundred million soldiers arrive on horseback!

THERE ARE TWO BASIC QUESTIONS ABOUT THESE RIDERS

Two questions need to be answered about this army. The first question revolves around the identity of these riders: Are they humans or demons?   Question two is as follows: Are we to understand their numbers literally or figuratively?

THE CASE FOR THE RIDERS BEING HUMAN

Many Bible commentators believe that Scripture is talking about a human army in this passage.

ARGUMENT 1: THIS IS THE SAME GROUP DESCRIBED IN REVELATION 16

Those who believe that a human army is in view here link this passage to the participants in the battle of Armageddon, as recorded in Revelation 16. However, imagining two huge armies gathered together, at two different times during the waning days of the "time of the end," seems to be impossible. Consequently, these two passages must be speaking about the same military conflict and the same participants.

ARGUMENT 2: THE EUPHRATES RIVERS IS EMPHASIZED IN EACH BATTLE

Another clue, which seemingly links these two passages and makes the case for a human army, is the Euphrates River. Since the river is mentioned in Revelation 9, as well as in Revelation 16; which, it is contended, is all fought by humans, it seems highly unlikely, if not impossible, to assume that two separate military battles take place at the time of the end with the Euphrates River highlighted in each one. Consequently, they must be one-in-the same battle.

ARGUMENT 3: THE POSSIBILITY OF A TWO HUNDRED MILLION MAN ARMY

When John wrote the Book of Revelation, it has been estimated that the population of the world was somewhere around two hundred million. In other words, there was no possible way that an army of that size could be mustered to fight a battle.

However, today, it is possible. Indeed, it has been estimated that China alone could field an army of 200 million. When put together with India, another possible ally, we find that there would be more than enough soldiers to come from the East to fight this battle.

ARGUMENT 4: THE LORD USES HUMAN ARMIES AS HIS INSTRUMENTS

Those who believe that this is a human army cite the numerous times in Scripture when God uses other suchlike heathen armies as instruments of His punishing of others.

ARGUMENT 5: THE WEAPONS MENTIONED ARE A FIRST CENTURY DESCRIPTION OF MODERN WEAPONS

The weapons described in verses 17-19 are John's best attempt to describe modern warfare, given the limitations of his vocabulary in the first century.

These arguments are used for those who contended that this is a literal battle with human beings who number 200 million. The great number is made up of "kings from the East" and is said to be the same campaign as Armageddon.

THE CASE FOR THE ARMY BEING DEMONIC

While many argue that the army in Revelation chapter 9 is made up of humans on horses, and that it should be linked to Armageddon, there are a number of reasons as to why others see it as a demonic army.

ARGUMENT 1: THE CONTEXT MAKES IT CLEAR THAT DEMONS ARE IN VIEW

In verses 2-10 of this same chapter, Revelation 9, we are introduced to demonic forces in the form of locusts. In other words, we previously have another description of a non-human army in this same context.

Furthermore, the two hundred-million-man army on horseback, in 9:16-19, has a number of things in common with the locust army previously mentioned. We find that both groups have breastplates, their tails inflict pain, and they have features like lions.

If the two groups are not identical, they are certainly closely related. Therefore, since the first group is obviously non-human, it naturally follows that this second group is likewise non-human.

ARGUMENT 2: THE NUMBER 200 MILLION IS NOT REALLY PLAUSIBLE

An army of 200 million men would not just consist of 200 million people. All armies need supply lines. When we start calculating what it would take to sustain such an army it seems to be an impossible undertaking. In other words, to mobilize such a force, as well as to supply it, does not appear to be realistic.

ARGUMENT 3: THE POPULATION OF THE WORLD HAS BEEN DEPLETED

Let us not forget that one fourth of the population of the world has previously been killed due to the judgment of the fourth seal:

> And I looked, and behold, a pale horse! And its rider's name was Death, and Hades followed him. And they were given authority over a fourth of the earth, to kill with sword and with famine and with pestilence and by wild beasts of the earth (Revelation 6:8 ESV).

Furthermore, the believers in Jesus Christ were previously removed from the world at the time of the rapture of the church. Their numbers also need to be subtracted from the inhabitants of the earth at this time.

ARGUMENT 4: THIS IS A DIFFERENT CONTEXT THAN ARMAGEDDON

We also find an entirely different context in Revelation 9 than in Revelation 16. Even though the Euphrates River is mentioned in each of these chapters, it is listed for different reasons.

ARGUMENT 5: DEATH IS INFLICTED BY THE HORSES NOT THE RIDERS

Another indication of the symbolic nature of this account is that death is inflicted upon the people by the horses, rather than the riders of the horses. In fact, the power to kill is in the mouth of the horses (Revelation 9:19).

CONCLUSION:

While a case certainly can be made for understanding the army of two hundred million as literal human beings, it may be better to see them as a demonic army that will kill one third of the people of the world.

THE PEOPLE STILL DO NOT REPENT

One last thing worth mentioning is that, even after the slaughter of one third of the inhabitants that are still upon the earth, the people still do repent of their sins:

> The rest of mankind who were not killed by these plagues still did not repent of the work of their hands; they did not stop worshiping demons, and idols of gold, silver, bronze, stone and wood—idols that cannot see or hear or walk. Nor did they repent of their murders, their magic arts, their sexual immorality or their thefts (Revelation 9:20-21 NIV).

The Seven Thunders, the Scroll, and the Ministry of the Two Witnesses (Revelation 10:1–11:14)

At this juncture, six of the seven trumpet judgments will have already taken place. Before the seventh trumpet blows, there is an interlude. It is during this interlude that certain other events will occur.

These following verses (Revelation 10:1–11:14) do not advance the narrative chronologically. Instead, we find more details added to the previous account. We also find that John will switch back and forth between heaven and earth in his description.

The scene begins with an angel descending from heaven:

> Then I saw another powerful angel descending from heaven, wrapped in a cloud, with a rainbow above his head; his face was like the sun and his legs were like pillars of fire. He held in his hand a little scroll that was open, and he put his right foot on the sea and his left on the land (Revelation 10:1-2 NET).

This scene sets us up for what is to immediately follow: the "seven thunders."

THE SEVEN THUNDERS

Immediately following the first couple of verses, we come to this fascinating event:

> Then he shouted in a loud voice like a lion roaring, and when
> he shouted, the seven thunders sounded their voices. When
> the seven thunders spoke, I was preparing to write, but just
> then I heard a voice from heaven say, "Seal up what the
> seven thunders spoke and do not write it down" (Revelation
> 10:3-4 NET).

For reasons known only to God, John was commanded to stop writing at this point. The fact that John was told not to write about these "seven thunders" has caused much speculation as to what he saw as well as why he was not allowed to write down his observations. However, since we have no idea as to what the seven thunders represented, all speculation is worthless.

THE COMPLETION OF ALL THINGS IS AT HAND

As the scene continues, the angel that descended from heaven now has an important announcement:

> Then the angel I saw standing on the sea and on the land
> raised his right hand to heaven and swore by the one who
> lives forever and ever, who created heaven and what is in it,
> and the earth and what is in it, and the sea and what is in
> it, "There will be no more delay! But in the days when the
> seventh angel is about to blow his trumpet, the mystery of
> God is completed, just as he has proclaimed to his servants
> the prophets" (Revelation 10:5-7 NET).

The end will not come before the seventh trumpet sounds, but it will come in association with it. In other words, the mystery of God will be fulfilled during the time of the seventh trumpet. God's plan to punish all evildoers, and to bring the kingdom of His Son to our world, is about to be accomplished!

JOHN EATS THE SCROLL

After the angelic announcement, another event takes place:

Then the voice I had heard from heaven began to speak to me again, "Go and take the open scroll in the hand of the angel who is standing on the sea and on the land." So I went to the angel and asked him to give me the little scroll. He said to me, "Take the scroll and eat it. It will make your stomach bitter, but it will be as sweet as honey in your mouth." So I took the little scroll from the angel's hand and ate it, and it did taste as sweet as honey in my mouth, but when I had eaten it, my stomach became bitter (Revelation 10:8-10 NET).

The voice from heaven commanded John to take the scroll from the angel who, in turn, instructed him to eat it. The results paralleled the bittersweet experience of the prophets Jeremiah and Ezekiel (Jeremiah 15:15-18, Ezekiel 2:8–3:3). These prophets proclaimed the Lord's truth to His people, Israel, but the people did not listen and judgment then came.

AN IMPORTANT LESSON: JOY MIXED WITH SADNESS

There is an important lesson for all of us in this "bittersweet moment." The joy of seeing God's Word accomplished is tempered by the overwhelming shock and sorrow related to the coming judgments. While believers should indeed rejoice that the kingdom of God is coming to the earth, at the same time we should not forget to think about the terrible consequences that the rebellious human race will experience.

THE INTERLUDE CONTINUES

Revelation 11:1-14 continues to fill in details before the sounding of the seventh trumpet. During this digression, the Bible records the appearance of two witnesses who arrive during the time of the end and testify to the truth of God's Word.

THE MINISTRY OF THE TWO WITNESSES

The Bible has the following to say about the ministry of these two witnesses:

> And I will appoint my two witnesses, and they will prophesy for 1,260 days, clothed in sackcloth. They are "the two olive trees" and the two lampstands, and "they stand before the Lord of the earth." If anyone tries to harm them, fire comes from their mouths and devours their enemies. This is how anyone who wants to harm them must die. They have power to shut up the sky so that it will not rain during the time they are prophesying; and they have power to turn the waters into blood and to strike the earth with every kind of plague as often as they want (Revelation 11:3-6 NIV).

They will stand up for God's truth for some three and one-half years. In doing so, they will exhibit supernatural powers which will be given to them directly from the Lord.

THE MURDER OF THE TWO WITNESSES

After their earthly ministry is complete, we are told that the beast, the final Antichrist, kills them. The Bible has the following to say:

> And when they have finished their testimony, the beast that rises from the bottomless pit will make war on them and conquer them and kill them, and their dead bodies will lie in the street of the great city that symbolically is called Sodom and Egypt, where their Lord was crucified. For three and a half days some from the peoples and tribes and languages and nations will gaze at their dead bodies and refuse to let them be placed in a tomb, and those who dwell on the earth will rejoice over them and make merry and exchange presents, because these two prophets had been a torment to those who dwell on the earth (Revelation 11:7-10 ESV).

The celebration goes on and on around the world.

THE TWO WITNESSES RETURN TO LIFE

However, the Bible says that a miracle then happens. Scripture tells us that these same two witnesses will be supernaturally brought back to life:

But after the three and a half days a breath of life from God entered them, and they stood up on their feet, and great fear fell on those who saw them. Then they heard a loud voice from heaven saying to them, "Come up here!" And they went up to heaven in a cloud, and their enemies watched them. And at that hour there was a great earthquake, and a tenth of the city fell. Seven thousand people were killed in the earthquake, and the rest were terrified and gave glory to the God of heaven (Revelation 11:10-13 ESV).

The Bible tells us that after this takes place, the two witnesses will be brought into heaven.

WHO ARE THESE TWO WITNESSES?

A number of questions arise about these two witnesses: Who are they? Are they real people who actually minister upon the earth in the last days, or are they merely symbolic of something else?

If they are real people, are they biblical characters from the past returning to the earth, or are they two contemporary people whom God inspires as His prophets?

OPTION 1: THE TWO WITNESSES ARE BIBLICAL CHARACTERS FROM THE PAST

A popular view is to see the two witnesses as biblical characters from the past. A number of suggestions have been given as to whom they might be.

MOSES

Moses is a likely candidate. For one thing, Moses was a prophet, therefore, he has the proper biblical credentials to speak out concerning what is taking place in these "last days."

In addition, Moses had the power to strike the earth with plagues. Using the power of the Lord, he turned the Nile River into blood. The two witnesses will have the power to do the same:

> They have power to shut up the sky so that it will not rain during the time they are prophesying; and they have power to turn the waters into blood and to strike the earth with every kind of plague as often as they want (Revelation 11:6 NIV).

Therefore, this miracle-working ability fits with what we know of the ability God gave to Moses.

Moreover, at Jesus' transfiguration, Moses appeared. He spoke with Jesus of things concerning the coming kingdom—the Second Coming of Christ. This may be another indication that Moses will appear shortly before Christ returns.

Interestingly, though Moses did die, we are told that the Lord Himself buried him. This may indicate that He had further plans for this prophet of God.

These things make Moses a likely candidate to be one of the two witnesses.

ELIJAH

Elijah is another popular candidate to be one of the two witnesses. There are a number of reasons as to why this is so.

For one thing, like Moses, Elijah was a prophet of God. Hence, he has the proper credentials to prophesy and do miracles in the name of the Lord.

Next, Elijah never experienced physical death. While death is not a requirement for every human being, it is possible he did not die because the Lord had plans for him to be one of the two witnesses.

Third, and what is even more significant, is that the Scripture expressly says that Elijah will come back to the earth before the return of the Lord:

See, I will send the prophet Elijah to you before that great
and dreadful day of the LORD comes (Malachi 4:5 NIV).

Fourth, Scripture speaks of Elijah calling fire down from heaven and
consuming a sacrifice in front of the false prophets of Baal. We read:

> And the water ran around the altar and even overflowed the
> trench. At the customary time for offering the evening sac-
> rifice, Elijah the prophet walked up to the altar and prayed,
> "O LORD, God of Abraham, Isaac, and Jacob, prove today
> that you are God in Israel and that I am your servant. Prove
> that I have done all this at your command. O LORD,
> answer me! Answer me so these people will know that you,
> O LORD, are God and that you have brought them back to
> yourself." Immediately the fire of the LORD flashed down
> from heaven and burned up the young bull, the wood, the
> stones, and the dust. It even licked up all the water in the
> ditch! (1 Kings 18:35-38 NLT).

As we have observed, one of the specific miracles attributed to the two
witnesses is the calling down of fire from heaven (Revelation 11:5).

Fifth, Elijah was given the ability to cause the land to be without rain
for a number of years. Again, this is one of the specific miracles attributed to the two witnesses.

Finally, at the Transfiguration of Jesus, Elijah appeared with Moses.

Many Bible students believe that the fact that Elijah and Moses
appeared together at the Transfiguration shows that they are the two
witnesses which will appear at the time of the end.

However, Moses and Elijah are not the only possible candidates among
the characters which we find on the pages of Scripture.

ENOCH

Another possibility is Enoch. The reason Enoch is preferred above Moses is that Enoch, like Elijah, did not die a physical death. The Bible says he left earth in the following way:

> Altogether, Enoch lived a total of 365 years. Enoch walked faithfully with God; then he was no more, because God took him away (Genesis 5:23-24 NIV).

Enoch did not die. Again, we emphasize that it is not necessary that every human being must die. In fact, an entire generation of believers will not experience physical death, but rather will be caught away into heaven at the rapture of the church.

Consequently, the fact that Enoch did not die does not necessarily make him one of the two witnesses. However, it does make him a prime candidate.

In addition, Enoch is also mentioned in the context of the return of the Lord. The Book of Jude notes that Enoch preached God's judgment before the Flood:

> Enoch, the seventh from Adam, prophesied about them: "See, the Lord is coming with thousands upon thousands of his holy ones to judge everyone, and to convict all the ungodly of all the ungodly acts they have done in an ungodly way, and of all the defiant words ungodly sinners have spoken against him" (Jude 14-15 NIV).

Enoch was a prophet of judgment, prophesying before the Lord sent the Flood of Noah to the world. Interestingly, Jesus compared the conditions at the time of His Second Coming to the conditions of the days of Noah.

> For as were the days of Noah, so will be the coming of the Son of Man. For as in those days before the flood they were

eating and drinking, marrying and giving in marriage, until the day when Noah entered the ark, and they were unaware until the flood came and swept them all away, so will be the coming of the Son of Man (Matthew 24:37-39 ESV).

Since Enoch pronounced judgment to come upon the earth the first time the entire world was judged, he may appear again to announce a "second" coming judgment of the world. Therefore, Enoch remains a viable candidate for one of the two witnesses.

OPTION 2: THE TWO WITNESSES ARE TWO MEN LIVING AT THE TIME OF THE EVENTS

It is possible, even likely, that if the two witnesses are literal human beings, they are two people from the Great Tribulation period who have qualities which were similar to Moses and Elijah. In other words, they are godly people who will be living on the earth at the time these events take place. God then chooses them to be His special witnesses to the earth.

Since the two witnesses are unnamed, and we would expect the return of Moses, Elijah or Enoch to be noted in Scripture if they were the two witnesses, then the idea that they are two people living at that time has much going for it.

OPTION 3: THE TWO WITNESSES ARE NOT LITERAL PEOPLE

Among those who do not interpret the Book of Revelation in a literal manner, are those who interpret the two witnesses as something symbolic, or not literal.

One of the problems with this interpretation, however, is that those who hold this view don't seem to agree about what these two witnesses are symbolic of.

THE WORD OF GOD: THE OLD AND NEW TESTAMENT

There are some who see these two witnesses as the Bible—the Old Testament and the New Testament. Yet this view breaks down when we try to interpret Revelation 11. The context calls for two human beings, not two testaments.

THE TWO PEOPLE OF GOD: ISRAEL AND THE CHURCH

Some see the two witnesses as representing the two people of God, the nation of Israel and the New Testament church. However, the same problems arise as with the previous possibility. The passage reads as though two human beings are in view, not Israel and the church.

CONCLUSION: NOBODY KNOWS THEIR IDENTITY FOR CERTAIN

The specific identity of these two witnesses has not been revealed to us. Any attempt to identify them is only speculation. It does, however, seem best to view the two witnesses as two actual people who perform this special ministry.

It also would not be inconsistent with the rest of Scripture to believe that the Lord actually brings Moses and Elijah back to earth for this ministry. However, it would also be in line with Scripture if we assume the two witnesses to be two godly people whom the Lord raises up, and who are living, at that time. Since we do not know the answer for certain, it is best that we hold our view with humility.

For more information on these two witnesses, as well as the events transpiring around their appearance, see our book *The Final Antichrist: The Coming Caesar.*

EVENT 16

The Seventh Trumpet Sounds
(Revelation 11:14, 15)

After the sounding of the sixth trumpet, the second "woe," we noted that there was a pause, or interlude (Event 15). We then find that the trumpet judgments are resumed in the eleventh chapter of the Book of Revelation, after the ministry of the "two witnesses" is complete.

This bring us to the blowing of the seventh trumpet, which is also connected with the third "woe." The Bible says:

> The second woe has passed; behold, the third woe is soon to come. Then the seventh angel blew his trumpet, and there were loud voices in heaven, saying, "The kingdom of the world has become the kingdom of our Lord and of his Christ, and he shall reign forever and ever" (Revelation 11: 14,15 ESV).

The seventh trumpet announces that the kingdom of the Lord is coming to the earth.

THE SCENE RETURNS TO HEAVEN

With the blowing of the seventh trumpet, the scene moves from the earth to heaven. Again, the twenty-four elders come into the picture:

> Then the twenty-four elders who are seated on their thrones before God threw themselves down with their faces to the

ground and worshiped God with these words: "We give you thanks, Lord God, the All-Powerful, the one who is and who was, because you have taken your great power and begun to reign. The nations were enraged, but your wrath has come, and the time has come for the dead to be judged, and the time has come to give to your servants, the prophets, their reward, as well as to the saints and to those who revere your name, both small and great, and the time has come to destroy those who destroy the earth (Revelation 11:16-18 NET).

As these elders give thanks to the Lord, we also find them testifying as to what has taken place as well as to what is about to occur.

The unbelieving nations have been angry at the Lord and have tried their best to prevent Jesus' coronation as the King of Kings. However, now the time has come for the Lord to be angry with them!

In other words, the destroyers are about to be destroyed; and, at the same time, the Lord is to reward His own servants, as well as His prophets, both the small and the great. Basically, the time for the final judgment of the earth is at hand.

THE TEMPLE OF GOD AND THE ARK OF THE COVENANT APPEAR IN HEAVEN

After we hear from the twenty-four elders, Scripture says that the Temple of God appears in heaven along with the Ark of the Covenant:

Then the temple of God in heaven was opened and the ark of his covenant was visible within his temple. And there were flashes of lightning, roaring, crashes of thunder, an earthquake, and a great hailstorm (Revelation 11:19 NET).

There are a couple of important observations that we should make from this event:

GOD'S TEMPLE IS THE TRUE HOLY TEMPLE

The Lord is emphasizing that there has been a holy Temple on the earth in the past, as there will be in the future (Isaiah 2:1-2, Ezekiel 40-48). We explain this further in Event 43: "The Millennial Temple." In the coming discussion of Event 43, we will find that the Temple that was built by Solomon was patterned after this one which now appears in heaven.

On the other hand, the Temple that is constructed during the Great Tribulation period will be an unholy one! In fact, it will be built as a rejection of Jesus Christ as the Messiah. As this rebuilt temple is about to be defiled with the arrival of the False Prophet, the Second Beast (see Event 18), the Lord is reminding His people of the Temple that He originally established. For more information on the subject of this future Temple, see our book *The Jews, Jerusalem, and the Coming Temple*.

THE ARK REPRESENTED THE PRESENCE OF THE LORD

The Ark of the Covenant was the most sacred object that has ever been constructed. It contained the Ten Commandments written by the "finger of God" and was delivered to Moses as he ascended Mt. Sinai. The Ark represented the presence of the Lord among His people.

The fact that the Ark in heaven shows up at this particular time is a further reminder of the meaning of the true Ark. Recall that the Ark constructed upon the earth had been made according to the pattern of the one in heaven.

It is also possible that the original Ark will be rediscovered and placed in the rebuilt Temple, the one built during the Great Tribulation period as a rejection of Jesus Christ. For more information on the subject of the Ark of the Covenant, see our book *In Search of the Lost Ark: The Quest for the Ark of the Covenant*.

A Great Sign In Heaven: Satan Is Cast Down to the Earth (Revelation 12)

The twelfth chapter is one of the most important in the entire Book of Revelation. In fact, to have a proper understanding of the time of the end, it is crucial that we understand the symbolism we find here as well as its meaning.

As we just emphasized, the eleventh chapter ended with an awesome sight in heaven. Scripture describes it as follows:

> Then God's temple in heaven was opened, and the ark of his covenant was seen within his temple. There were flashes of lightning, rumblings, peals of thunder, an earthquake, and heavy hail (Revelation 11:19 ESV).

THE GREAT SIGN

We are then told of a "great sign" that will appear in heaven:

> Then a great sign appeared in heaven: a woman clothed with the sun, and with the moon under her feet, and on her head was a crown of twelve stars. She was pregnant and was screaming in labor pains, struggling to give birth. Then another sign appeared in heaven: a huge red dragon that had seven heads and ten horns, and on its heads were seven diadem crowns. Now the dragon's tail swept away a third

of the stars in heaven and hurled them to the earth. Then the dragon stood before the woman who was about to give birth, so that he might devour her child as soon as it was born. So the woman gave birth to a son, a male child, who is going to rule over all the nations with an iron rod. Her child was suddenly caught up to God and to his throne, and she fled into the wilderness where a place had been prepared for her by God, so she could be taken care of for 1,260 days (Revelation 12:1-6 NET).

We have a number of things going on here.

First, a sign appears in heaven, a "great sign!" This should catch our attention. In fact, this is the only time this specific phrase is used in the Book of Revelation. So, it is obviously an attention-getter.

Next, there is the description of a pregnant woman who wears a crown of twelve stars. She is clothed with the sun with the moon under her feet. As she struggles to give birth, another sign appears in heaven—a red dragon with seven heads and ten horns. Finally, a male child, who will rule the nations, is born to the woman. What do all these symbols represent?

THE IDENTITY OF THE WOMAN

There have been a number of suggested identifications of the woman. They include the following:

MARY THE MOTHER OF JESUS

A popular view is that the woman is Mary, the mother of Jesus. This would be a literal understanding of the identity of the woman since Mary gave birth to Jesus, the One who will eventually rule. However, everything else in the entire context, except the male child, is symbolic.

Furthermore, this theory breaks down as we continue with this chapter.

Indeed, there was no persecution of Mary by the devil as is predicted here.

Also, Mary was not supernaturally protected from the devil for three and one-half years, or 1,260 days, as this woman will be.

THE CHURCH

Others think that the Church is in view. However, it did not, in any sense, bring forth Jesus. In fact, Jesus gave birth to the church!

Furthermore, there is nothing in the history of the church that would fulfill the prediction of the three-and-one-half year period of being supernaturally protected from the devil.

THE NATION OF ISRAEL

The best answer is that the woman is a description of the nation of Israel. This interpretation fits well with the symbols in the dream of Joseph the patriarch:

> Then he had another dream, and told it to his brothers. "Look," he said. "I had another dream. The sun, the moon, and eleven stars were bowing down to me." When he told his father and his brothers, his father rebuked him, saying, "What is this dream that you had? Will I, your mother, and your brothers really come and bow down to you?" (Genesis 37:9-10 NET).

The sun and the moon represent Joseph's parents—Jacob and Leah—and the eleven stars represented his brothers, Joseph would have been the twelfth.

Indeed, the woman we read of is the nation of Israel, which bore Jesus, the promised Messiah. In fact, Scripture emphasizes that Jesus is of Jewish descent:

> To them belong the patriarchs, and from them, by human descent, came the Christ, who is God over all, blessed forever! Amen (Romans 9:5 NET).

All in all, this is the best way to interpret the identity of the woman.

THE SECOND SIGN: THE RED DRAGON, THE DEVIL, WITH SEVEN HEADS AND TEN HORNS

There is certainly no problem in identifying the second sign—the red dragon. In fact, his identity is given to us later in this chapter:

> So that huge dragon—the ancient serpent, the one called the devil and Satan, who deceives the whole world—was thrown down to the earth, and his angels along with him (Revelation 12:9 NET).

Satan is the supernaturally created being who led an angelic rebellion against the Lord in the beginning.

He is the red dragon, the devil, who is described as having seven heads and ten horns. The seven heads likely symbolize the seven consecutive Gentile world empires of Revelation 17:10 which will have been under his control.

The ten horns, then, would then represent the evil confederacy of nations which will be aligned with the devil and the final Antichrist at the time of the end. The diadems seemingly speak of his political authority.

THE MALE CHILD IS JESUS

Another easy identification, which we touched upon when we identified the "woman" of this passage, is that of the male child. He is Jesus. In fact, before He was conceived, the angel Gabriel told Mary that He would rule on the throne of David over the house of Israel:

So the angel said to her, "Do not be afraid, Mary, for you have found favor with God! Listen: You will become pregnant and give birth to a son, and you will name him Jesus. He will be great, and will be called the Son of the Most High, and the Lord God will give him the throne of his father David. He will reign over the house of Jacob forever, and his kingdom will never end" (Luke 2:30-34 NET).

In addition, Scripture emphasizes the fact that Christ will rule upon His return:

Then I saw heaven opened, and there was a white horse. Its rider is called Faithful and True, and he judges and makes war with justice. . . . A sharp sword came from his mouth, so that he might strike the nations with it. He will rule them with an iron rod (Revelation 19:11,15 CSB).

THE DRAGON PERSECUTES THE JEWS

With the identity of the "woman," "red dragon," and "child" understood, we now can come to the last verse of our passage:

Then the woman fled into the wilderness, where she has a place prepared by God, that they should feed her there one thousand two hundred and sixty days (Revelation 12:6 NKJV).

Persecution of the Jews now begins. The Book of Daniel, in speaking of the time of the end, says:

As I looked, this horn made war with the saints and prevailed over them (Daniel 7:21 ESV).

In this context, the "saints" refer to the nation of Israel, the Jews. They are Satan's special target. This is not surprising since the devil has targeted the chosen people from the very beginning.

WAR BREAKS OUT IN HEAVEN: THE DRAGON IS CAST TO THE EARTH

Briefly, before we are given a more detailed account of the persecution of Israel, the Scripture shifts and we are given a glimpse of another heavenly scene. We find that Satan, who has always been allowed access to the Lord, will be thrown out of heaven along with his angels:

> Then war broke out in heaven: Michael and his angels fought against the dragon, and the dragon and his angels fought back. But the dragon was not strong enough to prevail, so there was no longer any place left in heaven for him and his angels. So that huge dragon-the ancient serpent, the one called the devil and Satan, who deceives the whole world-was thrown down to the earth, and his angels along with him (Revelation 12:7-10 ESV).

This is a tremendous event! In fact, we are told that it caused the heavens to rejoice.

SATAN ATTEMPTS TO DESTROY ISRAEL: GOD MIRACULOUSLY PROTECTS THEM

Not to be deterred by being cast down from heaven, the dragon then pursues the woman—Israel. The Bible says:

> When the dragon saw that he had been thrown down to the earth, he persecuted the woman who had given birth to the male child. The woman was given two wings of a great eagle, so that she could fly from the serpent's presence to her place in the wilderness, where she was nourished for a time, times, and half a time. From his mouth the serpent spewed water like a river flowing after the woman, to sweep her away with a flood. But the earth helped the woman. The earth opened its mouth and swallowed up the river that the dragon had spewed from his mouth (Revelation 12:13-16 CSB).

We also find another parallel with the Exodus. Moses wrote the following about the deliverance of Israel from Egypt after the Egyptian army drowned in the Red Sea:

> You stretch out your right hand, and the earth swallows your enemies. In your unfailing love you will lead the people you have redeemed. In your strength you will guide them to your holy dwelling (Exodus 15:12,13 NIV).

There are a number of important things that we learn from this passage.

THE WOMAN IS GIVEN THE WINGS OF THE GREAT EAGLE

As the woman, Israel, flees from the persecution of the dragon, she is given the ability to escape his clutches to her "place in the wilderness." The metaphor of her deliverance, the "wings of an eagle," was previously used regarding Israel's exodus from Egypt. The Lord said:

> You yourselves have seen what I did to Egypt and how I lifted you on eagles' wings and brought you to myself (Exodus 19:4 NET).

This is, yet, another indication that the woman represents Israel.

The Scripture also says that this "escape" to the wilderness will be for "time, and times, and half a time," mentioned in verse 14 (also Daniel 7:25). This is in reference to a three-and-one-half-year period during the Great Tribulation in which God will meet all of Israel's needs.

THE PEOPLE WILL BE PROTECTED: PETRA?

As we just mentioned, the nation will be supernaturally preserved by God in a wilderness location. Outside of the term "wilderness," Scripture does not say where the people will be protected during this three-and-one-half year period of time. It has been a popular view that they will be in the ancient city of Petra, in Jordan. However, Scripture does not specify the place.

WILL THE DEVIL LITERALLY CAUSE A FLOOD?

The devil will send a flood in an attempt to destroy the woman but the earth will open up and receive the water to protect Israel from destruction. There has been much discussion as to whether or not this is a literal flood.

Those who believe the flood is not literal point out that the term is likely used for enemies of Israel. This is consistent with the Old Testament use of the term. The psalmist wrote:

> Reach down your hand from on high; deliver me and rescue me from the mighty waters, from the hands of foreigners whose mouths are full of lies, whose right hands are deceitful (Psalm 144:7-8 NIV).

We have something similar recorded in Daniel:

> At the time of the end the king of the South will engage him in battle, and the king of the North will storm out against him with chariots and cavalry and a great fleet of ships. He will invade many countries and sweep through them like a flood (Daniel 11:40 NIV).

In other words, those who see the flood as being not literal see the enemies of Israel attempting to destroy them, but the Lord thwarting their efforts, just as is seen in the Old Testament Scriptures. Thus, the earth, that symbolically swallows up the waters of the flood, would signify the Lord's supernatural deliverance.

THE DEVIL ATTEMPTS TO DESTROY THOSE REMAINING FROM ISRAEL

After this supernatural deliverance takes place, the devil will then go after the "rest of her children:"

So the dragon became enraged at the woman and went away to make war on the rest of her children, those who keep God's commandments and hold to the testimony about Jesus. And the dragon stood on the sand of the seashore (Revelation 12:17,18 NET).

The "rest of her children" is best understood to be either people from the entire nation of Israel, or a believing remnant of the people who have placed their faith in Jesus as the Messiah during the Great Tribulation period.

The Arrival of the False Prophet, the Second Beast (Revelation 13)

After the Lord hurls Satan down to the earth, and miraculously protects Israel from the devil's attempt to destroy the nation, the focus comes upon two individuals—the "first and second beast." Since we have already documented the career of the "first beast," the final Antichrist (Event 9), we will now turn our attention to the "second beast."

This "second beast" arrives on the scene in the last days to promote the final Antichrist. He is also called the "false prophet."

The Bible explains him as follows:

> Then I saw another beast come up out of the earth. He had two horns like those of a lamb, but he spoke with the voice of a dragon. He exercised all the authority of the first beast. And he required all the earth and its people to worship the first beast, whose fatal wound had been healed. He did astounding miracles, even making fire flash down to earth from the sky while everyone was watching (Revelation 13:11-13 NLT).

This "second beast" looks like a lamb, but is, in point of fact, like a dragon. The dragon, as we saw in our previous event, is one of many symbols that represents the devil.

False prophets and false teachers have been around from the very beginning. These evil individuals always pervert the message of the God of the Bible. The Apostle John said there were many of these false prophets in his day. He wrote:

> Dear friends, do not believe every spirit, but test the spirits to determine if they are from God, because many false prophets have gone out into the world. By this you know the Spirit of God: Every spirit that confesses Jesus as the Christ who has come in the flesh is from God, but every spirit that does not confess Jesus is not from God, and this is the spirit of the antichrist, which you have heard is coming, and now is already in the world (1 John 4:1-3 CSB).

These particular false prophets that John wrote about denied that Jesus was a genuine human being. In other words, they denied His true humanity. This is consistent with all false prophets—they are always denying some essential truth of the Christian faith.

FALSE PROPHETS WILL CONTINUE UNTIL THE END

The Bible stresses the fact that false prophets will continue to emerge until the time of the end. Jesus warned that many false prophets would appear:

> For false christs and false prophets will arise and perform great signs and wonders, so as to lead astray, if possible, even the elect (Matthew 24:24 ESV).

Therefore, we should always expect to have false prophets among us.

THE ULTIMATE FALSE PROPHET, THE SECOND BEAST

Coming back to this "ultimate" or "final" false prophet that we've mentioned, we see that he is different. This evil individual will come onto the scene of history at the time of the end. He is called the "second beast" or "another beast." This makes it clear that the second beast is a different personage from the first beast—the man of sin, the final Antichrist. This second beast is introduced as follows:

> Then I saw another beast rising out of the earth. It had two horns like a lamb and it spoke like a dragon (Revelation 13:11 ESV).

Two things are immediately apparent about this "second beast." To begin with, he comes out of the earth. This could mean that his origin is from this world as opposed to heaven, or it could be emphasizing that he has no divine authority whatsoever.

There is also the possibility that this description is emphasizing that he is Jewish. The word "earth" could also be translated as "land." Consequently, the false prophet may actually come from the Promised Land and from the chosen people. Thus, he is Jewish. This would be in contrast with the first beast, who seemingly is a Gentile.

We are also told that this second beast looks like a harmless lamb, but speaks as a dragon. His appearance and speech make him appear to be not dangerous. Yet, in actuality, his words originate from the pit of hell.

Who, then, is this second beast? What exactly is the role of this false prophet in the end times? Scripture has the following to say:

THE SECOND BEAST IS CALLED "THE" FALSE PROPHET

On three occasions, the second beast is called "the false prophet." In each of these instances, he is aligned with the first beast—the man of sin, the final Antichrist.

We first read of this title "the false prophet" in the sixteenth chapter of the Book of Revelation, where it says the following:

> Then I saw three evil spirits that looked like frogs; they came out of the mouth of the dragon, out of the mouth of the

beast and out of the mouth of the false prophet (Revelation 16:13 NIV).

In this instance, evil spirits proceed from the dragon, Satan; the beast, Antichrist; as well as from the false prophet, this "second beast." These three personages are known as the "unholy trinity."

In another place of Scripture, we are told that the false prophet is captured,

along with the beast, at the time of the Second Coming of Jesus Christ to the earth. Scripture says:

> But the beast was captured, and with him the false prophet who had performed the signs on his behalf. With these signs he had deluded those who had received the mark of the beast and worshiped his image. The two of them were thrown alive into the fiery lake of burning sulfur (Revelation 19:20 NIV).

It is said, here, that "the false prophet" is thrown into the lake of fire.

One thousand years later we discover that he is still there:

> And the devil, who deceived them, was thrown into the lake of burning sulfur, where the beast and the false prophet had been thrown. They will be tormented day and night for ever and ever (Revelation 20:10 NIV).

These are the only three passages which specifically describe the second beast as the "false prophet."

WHO IS THE SECOND BEAST, THE FALSE PROPHET?

From the passages above, it is clear that the second beast is also called *the* false prophet. This brings up an obvious question. Who is this "second beast," "the" false prophet? From Scripture, we can make the following conclusions:

1. HE IS DISTINCT FROM THE FIRST BEAST AND THE DEVIL

The false prophet is distinct from the first beast. He is called the "second beast." This makes a clear distinction between this beast and the first beast. They are not the same personage.

His character and mission are also distinct from the first beast. While the first beast is more of a political and military leader, the false prophet will be a religious leader.

Furthermore, as we have just noted, the "second beast" is distinguished from the first beast and the devil in Revelation chapters nineteen and twenty. The beast and the false prophet are thrown into the lake of fire in chapter nineteen of the Book of Revelation, while the devil is not.

Later, in chapter twenty, we are told that the devil joins them in the lake of fire. Therefore, we can rightly conclude that the false prophet is a distinct personage from the first beast and the devil himself.

2. HE IS A MIRACLE WORKER

We also find that the second beast, the false prophet, works miracles. Scripture says:

> He did astounding miracles, even making fire flash down to earth from the sky while everyone was watching (Revelation 13:13 NLT).

In fact, he is a greater miracle worker than the first beast.

There is something we must note about his miracles, however. We are told that the false prophet mimics the two witnesses of Revelation 11 in their miraculous deeds.

Indeed, the same miracles which the Bible says the two witnesses perform are also performed by this false prophet. This includes calling fire down from heaven.

Such mimicking of God's miracles reminds us of the battle of Moses and Aaron with the magicians of the Pharaoh of Egypt. We find that the magicians were mimicking some of the miracles that the Lord performed through Moses and Aaron. This mimicking of the miracles is repeated by the deeds of the false prophet.

3. HE IS A SATANIC VERSION OF JOHN THE BAPTIST

The false prophet can be compared to a satanic version of John the Baptist. As John prepared the way for the genuine Messiah, the false prophet will point people to the false Messiah. In this sense, he is like a devilish version of John the Baptist. This second beast will be the chief promoter of the first beast.

4. HE WILL MAKE AN IMAGE OF THE FIRST BEAST

As the promoter of the first beast, he causes the people to make an image of him. The Bible says:

> And with all the miracles he was allowed to perform on behalf of the first beast, he deceived all the people who belong to this world. He ordered the people of the world to make a great statue of the first beast, who was fatally wounded and then came back to life (Revelation 13:14 NLT).

This image, or statue, is of the first beast who survived a seemingly fatal wound.

This act of sacrilege is called the "abomination of desolation" by Jesus:

> So when you see standing in the holy place 'the abomination that causes desolation,' spoken of through the prophet Daniel—let the reader understand (Matthew 24:15 NIV).

The image of the first beast will be placed in the Holy of Holies in the rebuilt temple in Jerusalem—the place designated only for the Holy Ark of the Covenant. This act will be the ultimate blasphemy against the God of Scripture.

5. HE IS ABLE TO GIVE LIFE TO THE STATUE OF THE FIRST BEAST

Somehow this final false prophet is able to perform a great miracle and give life to the statue, or image, that he made of the first beast. This image will also be able to speak! The Bible explains it this way:

> He was permitted to give a spirit to the image of the beast, so that the image of the beast could both speak and cause whoever would not worship the image of the beast to be killed (Revelation 13:15 CSB).

This seems to be an incredible miracle. We are not told how he is able to do it.

6. THE FALSE PROPHET CAUSES PEOPLE TO WORSHIP THE IMAGE OF THE BEAST

As the false prophet, he then causes people of the world to worship a false god, the first beast. The Bible says:

> The second beast was empowered to give life to the image of the first beast so that it could speak, and could cause all those who did not worship the image of the beast to be killed (Revelation 13:15 NET).

The false prophet will order the death of all who refuse to worship this image of the first beast.

7. HE MAKES PEOPLE TAKE THE MARK OF THE FIRST BEAST

We also find that all who worship the first beast will receive his mark. The false prophet is the one who enforces this. The Book of Revelation says:

> And he requires everyone — small and great, rich and poor, free and slave — to be given a mark on his right hand or on his forehead, so that no one can buy or sell unless he

has the mark: the beast's name or the number of his name (Revelation 13:16-17 CSB).

Those who refuse to worship the first beast are denied the right to buy and sell. In other words, they cannot do anything without the mark of the first beast. All of this is facilitated by the false prophet. Consequently, he is the one who ultimately controls the commerce of the world.

8. HE MAY BE THE ONE WHO BRINGS THE FIRST BEAST BACK TO LIFE

There is another matter which we should consider about this second beast. Though it is not directly stated in Scripture, it is possible that the false prophet is the one who brings the first beast—the final Antichrist—back to life after he receives a mortal head wound.

We are told that the first beast dies and then comes back to life. While not stated, it may be inferred that the second beast is the one who performs this miracle. Since the second beast, the false prophet, has the ability to give life to the statue of the first beast, it is not out of the question that he will be able to facilitate the resuscitation of the first beast.

Of course, all this has to happen under the control of God. These personages have no power, in-and-of-themselves, to give life to the dead.

9. THE FALSE PROPHET HAS THE SAME DESTINY AS SATAN AND THE FIRST BEAST

As the devil and the first beast will eventually be cast into the lake of fire, the false prophet, the second beast, will experience this same fate. The Bible says:

> Then the Devil, who betrayed them, was thrown into the lake of fire that burns with sulfur, joining the beast and the false prophet. There they will be tormented day and night forever and ever (Revelation 20:10 NLT).

Each of these despicable humans will suffer the same punishment (see Event 36).

A LOOK AT THE CHARACTER AND DEEDS OF THE SECOND BEAST, THE FALSE PROPHET

From a look at the Scripture, we find the following things said about the deeds and character of this second beast.

1. HE WILL MIMIC THE HOLY SPIRIT

As the Antichrist, the first beast, attempts to usurp the rightful place of Jesus Christ, God the Son; the second beast, the false prophet, will mimic the Third Person of the Trinity, the Holy Spirit.

2. HE WILL PROMOTE OR GLORIFY THE FIRST BEAST

One of the ways in which he will mimic the Holy Spirit is through his role to the first beast. The job of this final false prophet will be to glorify the first beast, he will not glorify himself. In this aspect, he will mimic the Holy Spirit.

Jesus said the ministry of the Holy Spirit is to testify to Him [Jesus], not of Himself. He said:

> When the Spirit of truth comes, he will guide you into all the truth, for he will not speak on his own authority, but whatever he hears he will speak, and he will declare to you the things that are to come. He will glorify me, for he will take what is mine and declare it to you (John 16:13-15 ESV).

The Holy Spirit teaches us about Jesus. In the same way, the false prophet will mimic the ministry of the Holy Spirit. However, the false prophet will lead people into error instead of the truth. He will encourage them to worship the false Christ.

3. HE WILL BUILD THE KINGDOM OF ANTICHRIST

As the Holy Spirit is the One who builds the church—the body of Christ— here upon the earth, it is the false prophet who builds the kingdom of Antichrist. This is another way in which this personage will mimic the work of God the Holy Spirit.

HE WILL BE THIRD PERSON OF THE UNHOLY GROUP OF THREE PERSONAGES

The false prophet, as we've previously mentioned, is part of an unholy group of three personal beings. Each one of them is individually mentioned in Revelation chapter twenty. Scripture says:

> And the devil who had deceived them was thrown into the lake of fire and sulfur where the beast and the false prophet were, and they will be tormented day and night forever and ever (Revelation 20:10 ESV).

This emphasizes that he is distinct from the first beast, who is called the Antichrist, as well as from the devil.

THE FALSE PROPHET BRINGS DEATH INSTEAD OF LIFE

The false prophet, this second beast, brings death instead of life. This is in contrast to the Holy Spirit of God who gives life. Indeed, we are told that it was the Spirit of God who raised Jesus from the dead. Paul wrote about this to the Romans:

> And if the Spirit of him who raised Jesus from the dead is living in you, he who raised Christ from the dead will also give life to your mortal bodies because of his Spirit who lives in you (Romans 8:11 NIV).

The contrast between God the Holy Spirit and this final false prophet, in this particular instance, is obvious—one brings life while the other brings death.

HE MARKS THOSE WHO BELONG TO ANTICHRIST

Last up in our discussion of the "second beast," *the* false prophet, is his role of marking those who worship the beast. We contrast his work with the Holy Spirit who "seals" or "marks" those who believe in Jesus. Paul wrote:

> In him you also, when you heard the word of truth, the gospel of your salvation, and believed in him, were sealed with the promised Holy Spirit, who is the guarantee of our inheritance until we acquire possession of it, to the praise of his glory (Ephesians 1:13-14 ESV).

As the Lord "marks" or "seals" His people, we read that the devil will do the same.

These are some of the things which we learn about the second beast of the Book of Revelation—*the* false prophet. Like the first beast, this second beast is completely and thoroughly evil. For more information on these two "beasts," see our book *The Final Antichrist: The Coming Caesar.*

The Mark of the Beast: 666
(Revelation 13:16-17)

In the thirteenth chapter of the Book of Revelation we are told about one of the things which is forced upon the people who live in the world shortly before the Second Coming of Christ. This "thing" we speak of is the "mark of the beast," a mark that each individual must take in order to be able to buy or sell. John wrote:

> He [the false prophet] also caused everyone (small and great, rich and poor, free and slave) to obtain a mark on their right hand or on their forehead. Thus no one was allowed to buy or sell things unless he bore the mark of the beast-that is, his name or his number (Revelation 13:16-17 NET).

Scripture says that the false prophet, the second beast, then forces everyone to receive a particular "mark of the beast." Nobody is exempt. The Bible says the following:

1. THE FALSE PROPHET IS THE PERSONAGE WHO INSTITUTES AND ENFORCES THIS MARK

The promoter of the first beast, this second beast, the false prophet, is the one who enforces this mark. He is the one who makes everyone receive this mark. It is not done by the final Antichrist, himself.

2. IT MAY BE SOME TYPE OF PHYSICAL MARK

Though we are not specifically told, the mark of the beast may be some type of physical image which is placed upon each person who receives it. In other words, it may be readily observable with the naked eye. If so, then it does not seem to be some type of computer chip which is implanted underneath the skin. Seemingly, everyone will be able to immediately see the mark.

However, we certainly cannot be confident of this. It is possible that it will be invisible to the naked eye. We just do not know enough to be certain about this.

3. THE MARK WILL BE PLACED UPON EITHER THE RIGHT HAND OR FOREHEAD

The next thing we learn about the mark is the placement of it. It will go on either the right hand or the forehead of the person. As we just mentioned, this will seemingly make it obvious to everyone whether or not someone has this particular mark. Apparently, it will be in plain sight.

4. EVERYONE HAS TO RECEIVE THIS MARK TO BUY OR SELL

Scripture is also clear that everyone has to receive this mark, there are no exceptions. Rich or poor, young or old, everyone must have it. Without this mark, there would be no buying or selling. In other words, no commerce whatsoever.

5. ONCE ON, IT CANNOT BE REMOVED FROM THE PERSON

Once the mark of the beast has been given to a person, it *cannot* be removed. It remains upon that person as long as they are alive. In other words, it is a *permanent* mark.

6. THE MARK IS A NUMBER

The Bible says that the mark constitutes a specific number. It is 666. No other mark or tattoo will be acceptable. It must be the 666.

7. IT IS THE NUMBER OF THE FIRST BEAST, THE MAN OF SIN

We also find that this mark is the number of the name of the first beast, the Final Antichrist. In some way, this number is linked to him.

8. THE MARK IS A SIGN OF OWNERSHIP

Receiving the mark, the brand of the beast, indicates ownership. Scripture gives examples of God marking certain people.

For example, the Lord marked Cain. We read about this in the Book of Genesis:

> Then the LORD put a mark on Cain to warn anyone who might try to kill him (Genesis 4:15 NLT).

In this instance, it was a mark of protection.

In addition, during the great tribulation period, the Lord will mark 144,000 separate individuals who will be His witnesses:

> After this I saw four angels standing at the four corners of the earth, holding back the four winds of the earth to prevent any wind from blowing on the land or on the sea or on any tree. Then I saw another angel coming up from the east, having the seal of the living God. He called out in a loud voice to the four angels who had been given power to harm the land and the sea: "Do not harm the land or the sea or the trees until we put a seal on the foreheads of the servants of our God." Then I heard the number of those who were sealed: 144,000 from all the tribes of Israel (Revelation 7:1-4 NIV).

This will also be a mark of protection and ownership—they belong to Him.

As the Lord marks His people, the beast will also mark his own. It is a parody of what God has done in the past, and will do during this same tribulation period. This is another way in which this man of sin mimics the Lord.

MANY PEOPLE WILL REFUSE TO ACCEPT THE MARK

We know from Scripture that there will be a number of people who will refuse to take this "mark of the beast." The Book of Revelation says:

> I saw thrones on which were seated those who had been given authority to judge. And I saw the souls of those who had been beheaded because of their testimony about Jesus and because of the word of God. They had not worshiped the beast or his image and had not received his mark on their foreheads or their hands. They came to life and reigned with Christ a thousand years (Revelation 20:4 NIV).

These people will pay with their lives. Yet this is a small price to pay to be able to spend eternity with the Lord.

This briefly sums up what the Scripture has to say about the "mark of the beast." For more information on the "mark of the beast" and this coming "man of sin," see our book *The Final Antichrist: The C oming Caesar.*

The Persecution and the Murder of the Tribulation Saints (Revelation 14)

During this time of the Great Tribulation, there will be the murder of many of the people who have turned to the Lord in faith. These people are known as the "tribulation saints."

THEY ARE A DISTINCT GROUP FROM THE CHURCH

It is important to understand that the "tribulation saints" are a distinct group from the New Testament church. The church is made up of the believers in Jesus Christ from the time of the Day of Pentecost until the catching up of believers to meet the Lord in the air—the rapture of the church (see Event 2). Once this event takes place, and the rapture is now past, those new to Jesus Christ become part of this next group—the tribulation saints. They are given this name because they come to faith in Christ during the Great Tribulation period.

THE ANTICHRIST WAGES WAR ON THE TRIBULATION SAINTS

During this time, the man of sin, the first beast, will wage an all-out war on the people of God. The Bible describes it as follows:

> This means that God's holy people must endure persecution patiently, obeying his commands and maintaining their faith in Jesus. And I heard a voice from heaven saying, "Write this down: Blessed are those who die in the Lord from now on.

> Yes, says the Spirit, they are blessed indeed, for they will rest
> from their hard work; for their good deeds follow them!"
> (Revelation 14:12,13 NLT).

Indeed, the final Antichrist will persecute those who have come to faith in Jesus during this period—they are known as the "tribulation saints." In other words, he attempts to destroy all those who belong to the Lord.

THE SOULS UNDER THE ALTAR

Earlier in the Book of Revelation, these believers who were martyred for their faith were referred to as the "souls of those under the altar:"

> When the Lamb broke the fifth seal, I saw under the altar the
> souls of all who had been martyred for the word of God and
> for being faithful in their testimony (Revelation 6:9 NLT).

From these two passages (Revelation 14:12,13 and Revelation 6:9), we also discover that those who believe in Christ are also singled out.

As we have already observed by looking at Event 17, the Jews will be singled out for persecution.

Consequently, there are two, and only two, people groups that these two beasts, the Antichrist and the False Prophet, persecute during the Great Tribulation period—the Jews and the believers in Jesus Christ.

The persecution of the Jews and Christians by the devil and his followers has been historically true, and it will remain true until the end.

The Fall of Babylon
(Revelation 14, 17, 20)

In Event 12, we saw the description of the 144,000 in Revelation 7, as well as in Revelation 14.

We noted, there, that Revelation 14 places us at a future time when the Lord returns from heaven. It is after this description, now, that three angels are introduced, each appearing with a proclamation. It is in the announcement of the second angel that a "great city" is mentioned:

> A second angel followed the first, declaring: "Fallen, fallen is Babylon the great city! She made all the nations drink of the wine of her immoral passion" (Revelation 14:8 NET).

The words "fallen, fallen is Babylon the great city" are anticipating its destruction. The details are given to us later in Revelation 17:1–18:24.

The subject of Babylon is vast. Indeed, entire books have been written about Babylon, its identity, and how it relates to the events of the "end times."

Accordingly, we will merely give a summary of some of the more important details of this coming event—the fall of Babylon.

WHO IS BABYLON?

The first question is obvious: Who or what is Babylon in the Book of Revelation? Bible students have not come to any definitive conclusion as to the identity of Babylon. Basically, four views have been prominent. They include the following:

OPTION 1: ROME

A popular view is that Babylon is actually a reference to first-century Rome. This view has a number of variations.

There are some commentators who argue that the early Christians used the code word "Babylon" to keep certain truths secret from Rome due to its persecution of believers. For example, Peter wrote:

> She who is at Babylon, who is likewise chosen, sends you greetings, and so does Mark, my son (1 Peter 5:13 ESV).

According to this view, when Peter mentioned Babylon he was referring to Rome. It is further contended that those who received this letter from Peter knew that he was not referring to literal Babylon while non-Christians would not have understood the secret meaning of the reference.

In this verse, Peter also mentions that John Mark was with him. Paul had placed John Mark in Rome on an earlier occasion (Colossians 4:10). Therefore, it is argued that John Mark was still in Rome at the time 1 Peter was written.

Add to this, almost all modern interpreters of First Peter believe that Babylon, in this instance, was a code name for Rome.

In addition, tradition says that Peter was executed near Rome which makes this reference to Rome even more likely.

It is also contended that John, who wrote the book of Revelation, would not dare speak openly against Rome. Therefore, he too applied the code name "Babylon" to this enemy of God's people.

Others say that "Babylon," in the Book of Revelation, stands for "future Rome"—the city which will be at the center of the worldwide apostasy in the "last days" (see Revelation 14:8, 16:19, 17:5, 18:2, 10, 21).

RESPONSE

Those who reject that Babylon is actually Rome usually argue as follows:

First, there is no evidence that at this time "Babylon" was used as some code word for Rome. In fact, First Peter contains nothing that would have been considered subversive to the Roman state at that time. Therefore, there would have been no need to give it the code name "Babylon."

While John Mark was at Rome on an earlier occasion, it does not necessarily follow that he remained there. Recall, he had an itinerant ministry like Paul and Peter.

Furthermore, to argue that John, who was banished to the Isle of Patmos by the authority of Rome, would have been fearful to use its name in referring to present or future events, ignores the fact that Revelation is a book that is from, as well as about, Jesus Christ. It is *His* revelation! Indeed, John was merely told to write down the things that he saw.

Finally, there were many Jews who were living in Babylon at the time that Peter wrote. Therefore, it is possible that this reference could be understood literally.

In sum, while "Babylon" may have been a code word for Rome for those in the early church, the evidence is certainly not decisive.

OPTION 2: JERUSALEM

There is also the view that "Babylon" refers to the city of Jerusalem. It is viewed as a city set against God and will be the object of His judgment.

RESPONSE

The problem with this view is that Scripture generally aligns Jerusalem with the Lord while Babylon is *always* aligned against Him.

Furthermore, there is no specific reference in Scripture where the city of Jerusalem is called "Babylon."

OPTION 3: THE ENTIRE WORLD SYSTEM

Another popular view is that Babylon symbolizes the evil world system which is set against God. This would include all of the major cities in the world.

RESPONSE

While it is true that the evil world system is constantly at odds with the plan and program of God, it seems that Babylon in this context has a more specific identification.

OPTION 4: BABYLON ON THE EUPHRATES

The final option sees "Babylon" referring to the rebuilt city of Babylon. In other words, "Babylon" literally means Babylon!

ARGUMENTS AGAINST A LITERAL BABYLON

The main argument against this view is that the prophecies of Babylon's final destruction (Isaiah 13:19-22; Jeremiah 51:24-26) were fulfilled during the sixth century B.C. Therefore, as far as Scripture is concerned, the city of Babylon is gone forever.

RESPONSE

The arguments against a literal interpretation of Babylon are not convincing. There are several reasons as to why this is so.

SOME DETAILS HAVE NEVER BEEN LITERALLY FULFILLED

There are a number of the details contained in these prophecies in Isaiah and Jeremiah, with respect to Babylon, that have never been fulfilled. Consequently, one must look to the future for their literal fulfillment.

ZECHARIAH WAS WRITTEN AFTER BABYLON FELL

In addition, there is Zechariah 5:5-11, which was written at least 20 years *after* the fall of Babylon in 539 B.C. In this chapter, Zechariah looks forward to a future building of an idolatrous shrine in the land of Shinar—another name for Babylon (Genesis 10:10). In other words, Babylon, as far as God's program is concerned, is not finished.

In sum, there are good commentators who hold each of these four views. Our view is that "Babylon" is the literal city of Babylon, which shall be rebuilt and then rise to power for a short time in the "last days."

With several different views possible, what we do know is this: whatever Babylon turns out to be, it will be destroyed by the Lord at His coming.

THE TIMING OF THE DESTRUCTION OF BABYLON

Chapters 17 and 18 of the Book of Revelation record the destruction of Babylon. There is some question as to the exact timing of the fall of this great city.

OPTION 1: THE DESTRUCTION OCCURS AT THE BEGINNING OF THE SEVEN-YEAR PERIOD

One view holds that these events in Revelation 17 and 18 do not chronologically follow Chapter 16, but rather they take place at the beginning of the final seven-year period.

OPTION 2: THE DESTRUCTION OCCURS AT THE END OF THE SEVEN-YEAR PERIOD

However, most commentators believe that the destruction of Babylon will occur at the end of the final seven-year period. In this instance, Revelation Chapter 14 looks forward to what will take place at the time of the Lord's return while Chapters 17 and 18 do indeed follow chronologically after Chapter 16.

THE DESTRUCTION OF BABYLON: THE ANTICHRIST WILL BREAK THE AGREEMENTS HE MADE

Since the final Antichrist is the ultimate liar, he will break the agreements and various alliances which he had previously made. This will include those he made with Babylon.

Antichrist will only use Babylon to gain his worldwide power. Once this is accomplished, Babylon will be done away with. The ten-nation confederation, which will be under his control, will destroy Babylon, which is also called the "harlot" or "prostitute." The Bible says:

> The beast and the ten horns you saw will hate the prostitute. They will bring her to ruin and leave her naked; they will eat her flesh and burn her with fire. For God has put it into their hearts to accomplish his purpose by agreeing to give the beast their power to rule, until God's words are fulfilled (Revelation 17:16–17 NIV).

The ten kings, who are under the control of the beast—the final Antichrist—will destroy Babylon. This reveals that it was foolish to place any trust in this man of sin.

THE ENEMIES OF THE LORD ARE DESTROYED

To sum up, whatever Babylon refers to, whether it be Rome, the evil worldwide system, or the ancient city of Babylon, it will be destroyed at the time of the end. Its worldwide dominance will be short-lived.

The Pronouncement of Judgement Against Those Who Have Take the Mark of the Beast: Eternal Punishment (Revelation 14:9-11)

In the midst of the angelic pronouncement of the judgment upon Babylon (detailed in the last event), the Lord gives a warning to those who personally receive the "mark of the beast:"

> A third angel followed the first two, declaring in a loud voice: "If anyone worships the beast and his image, and takes the mark on his forehead or his hand, that person will also drink of the wine of God's anger that has been mixed undiluted in the cup of his wrath, and he will be tortured with fire and sulfur in front of the holy angels and in front of the Lamb. And the smoke from their torture will go up forever and ever, and those who worship the beast and his image will have no rest day or night, along with anyone who receives the mark of his name" (Revelation 14:9-11 NET).

This is an awesome pronouncement. Indeed, it predicts the horrible, eternal destiny of those who reject Jesus Christ as Savior.

THE DOCTRINE OF ETERNAL PUNISHMENT

Since this pronouncement is highlighted in Scripture as one of the important "last days" events, we need to say a few words about what exactly it is describing—eternal punishment.

Those who receive the "mark of the beast" will experience the wrath of God. Indeed, they will be punished forever in the presence of the Lord; this is clear. Furthermore, there is no relief from that punishment—it is day and night and it is everlasting.

While this passage is speaking specifically of those who take the mark during the Great Tribulation period, it is consistent with the rest of Scripture which teaches the doctrine of everlasting punishment of all those who reject the Lord.

As we shall now see, the Book of Revelation provides further support for the doctrine of the everlasting punishment of the wicked.

THE BEAST AND THE FALSE PROPHET ARE THROWN INTO THE LAKE OF FIRE

When Jesus Christ returns to the earth, He will capture the beast and the false prophet and cast them both alive into the lake of fire:

> But the beast was captured, and with it the false prophet who had performed the signs on its behalf. With these signs he had deluded those who had received the mark of the beast and worshiped its image. The two of them were thrown alive into the fiery lake of burning sulfur (Revelation 19:20 NIV).

Notice they are thrown alive into the lake of fire. There is nothing said about their extinction, or annihilation, when they receive this punishment. Indeed, this punishment is eternal—everlasting.

THE DESTINY OF THE DEVIL

One thousand years later, we find that the created spirit-being, who became the devil, will also be thrown into the same lake of fire as the beast and false prophet:

> When the thousand years are over, Satan will be released from his prison and will go out to deceive the nations in

the four corners of the earth . . . And the devil, who deceived them, was thrown into the lake of burning sulfur, where the beast and the false prophet had been thrown. They will be tormented day and night for ever and ever (Revelation 20:7,10 NIV).

We should observe here that the beast and false prophet are still in the lake of fire one thousand years after they had previously been cast into this fiery punishment. In other words, they have been tormented all of this time—burned, but not consumed.

THE GREAT WHITE THRONE JUDGMENT

Finally, we come to the Last Judgment, also known as the Great White Throne. This is indeed an awesome scene:

Then I saw a great white throne and him who was seated on it. The earth and the heavens fled from his presence, and there was no place for them. And I saw the dead, great and small, standing before the throne, and books were opened. Another book was opened, which is the book of life. The dead were judged according to what they had done as recorded in the books. The sea gave up the dead that were in it, and death and Hades gave up the dead that were in them, and each person was judged according to what they had done. Then death and Hades were thrown into the lake of fire. The lake of fire is the second death. Anyone whose name was not found written in the book of life was thrown into the lake of fire (Revelation 20:11-15 NIV).

In this final judgment, those whose names are not found written in the Book of Life are thrown into the lake of fire, the same lake of fire where the devil, the beast, and the false prophet have already been cast into.

The destiny of those who do not believe in Christ is the same as these three personages—they are forever separated from the Lord in a place of conscious punishment.

THE UNRIGHTEOUS REMAIN OUTSIDE OF THE HOLY CITY

After this "last judgment," the Lord then creates a "new heaven" and a "new earth." The "Holy City," the "New Jerusalem," comes down from heaven to the new earth.

In the explanation of the New Jerusalem, we find that the unbelievers exist "outside" of the presence of the Lord. We also discover that they will remain there forever. Three passages make this clear:

> The one who conquers will inherit these things, and I will be his God and he will be my son. But to the cowards, unbelievers, detestable persons, murderers, the sexually immoral, and those who practice magic spells, idol worshipers, and all those who lie, their place will be in the lake that burns with fire and sulfur. That is the second death (Revelation 21:7,8 NET).

First, it is re-emphasized that the lost are in the lake of fire.

Then we are told that *only* the righteous will be able to enter the Holy City:

> They will bring the grandeur and the wealth of the nations into it, but a nothing ritually unclean will ever enter into it, nor anyone who does what is detestable or practices falsehood, but only those whose names are written in the Lamb's book of life (Revelation 21:26 NET).

While individuals from the various nations will enter the New Jerusalem, the entrance is limited. Indeed, only those whose names are written in the Book of Life may enter the Holy City. The unbelievers will *never* be able to enter into it.

Later, the same thing is repeated:

> Blessed are those who wash their robes so they can have access to the tree of life and can enter into the city by the

gates. Outside are the dogs and the sorcerers and the sexually immoral, and the murderers, and the idolaters and everyone who loves and practices falsehood! (Revelation 22:14 NET).

For a third time, we are told that only the righteous have access to the Holy City. Outside of the New Jerusalem are the unbelievers. They will remain outside forever.

Therefore, in these three verses, we are told that the fate of the wicked will be in the lake of fire—the "second" death or "eternal" death. They will never be able to enter the Holy City; they will always remain outside.

SUMMARY OF THE PUNISHMENT OF THE LOST

From the last book of the Bible—Revelation—we find further information about the fate of the lost. Indeed, in this particular book there are a number of passages which clearly state the destiny of the wicked, as well as the devil who has deceived them.

CONCLUSION: THE WICKED WILL BE ETERNALLY PUNISHED

In sum, from the totality of biblical teaching, there is no doubt whatsoever that the wicked will be judged, and then after their judgment comes the punishment, the payback, for not accepting the truth of God as revealed in the Bible. Their punishment will be eternal and conscious. This is the consistent teaching of Scripture on the subject.

For more information about this subject of the punishment of the wicked, see our book *Hell: The Final Destination of the Wicked.*

The Final Plagues, the Bowls of Wrath (Revelation 15)

We now come to the time when the final plagues are about to be completed. The Bible gives us this announcement:

> Then I saw another great and astounding sign in heaven: seven angels who have seven final plagues (they are final because in them God's anger is completed) (Revelation 15:1 NET).

This is an important announcement of what is about to come. It tells us several things.

First, it is described in superlatives—"a great and astounding sign." In other words, this particular sign is especially important.

Next, it reiterates that this is a time of the wrath of God upon the Christ-rejecting world. Indeed, this entire time, as recorded in Revelation 6-18, is the period where God's wrath will be poured out on an unbelieving world.

Third, there is a finality to God's judgment. With these final seven plagues, the end will come.

VICTORY FOR THE SAINTS: ANOTHER LINK TO THE EXODUS

In the next couple of verses, we see those who have died for the cause of Jesus Christ during this period—the tribulation saints—singing the song of Moses (Exodus 15:1-18). We read:

> I also saw something like a sea of glass mixed with fire, and those who had won the victory over the beast, its image, and the number of its name, were standing on the sea of glass with harps from God. They sang the song of God's servant Moses and the song of the Lamb: Great and awe-inspiring are your works, Lord God, the Almighty; just and true are your ways, King of the nations. Lord, who will not fear and glorify your name? For you alone are holy. All the nations will come and worship before you because your righteous acts have been revealed (Revelation 15:3-4 CSB).

This is the same song that the children of Israel sang after they were supernaturally delivered from Egypt and passed through the Red Sea. Again, we see another link between the events that will take place in the future and the Exodus of the children of Israel from Egypt. Of course, none of this is coincidental.

THE TEMPLE OPENED IN HEAVEN

Next, we see the temple opened in heaven:

> After these things I looked, and the temple (the tent of the testimony) was opened in heaven, and the seven angels who had the seven plagues came out of the temple, dressed in clean bright linen, wearing wide golden belts around their chests. Then one of the four living creatures gave the seven angels seven golden bowls filled with the wrath of God who lives forever and ever, and the temple was filled with smoke from God's glory and from his power. Thus no one could enter the temple until the seven plagues from the seven angels were completed (Revelation 15:5-8 NET).

In this passage, John sees the heavenly tabernacle of testimony opened. The seven angels, who had the seven plagues, emerge with garments of linen and golden sashes. Their clothing represents the righteousness of God.

THE BOWLS OF WRATH

These seven angels, described above, are holding golden bowls which represent the wrath of God. These vessels may be intended to bring to mind those which were used in the Temple in the Old Testament:

> Solomon also made all these items for the Lord's temple . . .
> the pure gold bowls . . . (1 Kings 7:48,50 NET).

We also find that nobody in the vision could stand in the presence of the Lord. Indeed, His fierce anger is about to be expressed on an unbelieving world.

The final plagues are about to occur. The wrath of God will soon be completed against a Christ-rejecting world.

The First Five Bowl Judgments
(Revelation 16:1-11)

This final group of judgments that the Lord will bring upon the earth are known as the "bowl" judgments. Like the "trumpet" judgments and the "seal" judgments, there are seven of them.

THEY BEAR SOME SIMILARITY TO THE TRUMPET JUDGMENTS

As we examine these bowl judgments, we discover that they bear certain similarities to the trumpet judgments. However, there is also a significant difference between them.

THEY ARE UNIVERSAL IN SCOPE

The impact of the trumpet judgments will affect only one-third of the planet (Revelation 8:7-8), while the impact of the bowl judgments will be universal in scope. Indeed, we read the following:

> Then the second angel poured out his bowl on the sea, and it became like the blood of a corpse. And everything in the sea died. Then the third angel poured out his bowl on the rivers and springs, and they became blood . . . Then the thunder crashed and rolled, and lightning flashed. And a great earthquake struck—the worst since people were placed on the earth (Revelation 16:3-4,18 NLT).

Hence, the trumpet judgments and the bowl judgments are best seen as two separate groups of punishments that the Lord delivers to the earth.

THEIR RESEMBLANCE TO THE PLAGUES IN EXODUS

It has also been observed that these bowl judgments, like the trumpet judgments, also bear a resemblance to the plagues that the Lord brought upon Egypt, as recorded in the Book of Exodus.

THE FIRST BOWL: PAINFUL SORES STRIKE THE PEOPLE OF THE EARTH (16:1-2)

This third and final series of punishments from the Lord—the bowl judgments—will be initiated by a command from heaven. What each of them will have in common is that they will be divinely planned and divinely orchestrated events. In other words, they will *not* be natural disasters.

This first plague is reminiscent of what took place in Egypt. We read:

> Then I heard a loud voice from the temple saying to the seven angels, "Go and pour out the seven bowls of God's wrath on the earth." The first went and poured out his bowl on the earth, and severely painful sores broke out on the people who had the mark of the beast and who worshiped its image (Revelation 16:1-2 CSB).

The pouring out of the first bowl will result in ulcerated sores for those living upon the earth—those who have taken the mark of the beast and who have worshipped his image.

> This reminds us of what took place in Egypt—the painful boils that struck the Egyptians (Exodus 9:9-11).

THE SECOND BOWL: THE SEA IS TURNED TO BLOOD

The second bowl also reminds us of what occurred in Egypt, before the Exodus. We read:

The second poured out his bowl into the sea. It turned to blood like that of a dead person, and all life in the sea died (Revelation 16:3 CSB).

This substance, that will be poured out by the angel, will turn all the seas in the world into blood. This will result in the death of *all* marine life living upon the face of the earth.

As we observed with the second trumpet judgment, recorded in Revelation 8:8-9, only one-third of the sea creatures will die at the time it takes place. In this instance of the second bowl, however, all creatures of the sea will perish.

This second bowl judgment is reminiscent of the Lord turning the water into blood in front of Pharaoh (Exodus 7:17-21).

THE THIRD BOWL: THE FRESH WATER IS TURNED TO BLOOD (16:4-7)

Next, the Lord will turn the fresh waters of the earth into blood:

The third poured out his bowl into the rivers and the springs of water, and they became blood (Revelation 16:4 CSB).

Basically, this punishment is similar to what happened with the sea; and, again, reminds us of what took place in Egypt (Exodus 7:17-21).

THE LORD DEMANDS BLOOD FOR BLOOD

After the first two bowl judgments, and the introduction of this third, the Apostle John heard certain words spoken which were associated with this third bowl. The Lord is praised as being eternal, holy, as well as righteous. This last attribute, His righteousness, will be directly related to His decision to punish those who persecuted His people during this period of Great Tribulation.

Since the inhabitants of the earth have poured out the blood of the believers in Jesus Christ, as well as the blood of the prophets, it is poetic justice that they themselves will be destroyed by means of blood.

Therefore, the punishment which these earth-dwellers will receive will be "blood for blood."

WE MUST REMEMBER THE EVIL PEOPLE DESERVED THE PUNISHMENT

The people who are punished are consistently portrayed as rejecting the Lord as well as persecuting and murdering His people. In other words, they deserve the punishment they are about to receive.

THE FOURTH BOWL: THE EARTH IS SCORCHED (16:8-9)

The fourth bowl affects the sun:

> The fourth poured out his bowl on the sun. It was allowed to scorch people with fire, and people were scorched by the intense heat. So they blasphemed the name of God, who has the power over these plagues, and they did not repent and give him glory (Revelation 16:8-9 CSB).

Previously, all of the water upon the earth had become blood and was, therefore, completely useless to drink. Now the fourth bowl will make the sun burn with inordinate heat, which will scorch the people of the earth. One can only imagine the intense agony that will come with this dreadful punishment.

Amazingly, the unbelieving people who remain upon the earth do not repent of their sins. Instead, they will continue to speak slanderously against the Lord.

THE FIFTH BOWL: THE EARTH IS PLUNGED INTO DARKNESS (16:10-11)

Darkness now comes upon the earth with the pouring out of the fifth bowl:

The fifth poured out his bowl on the throne of the beast, and its kingdom was plunged into darkness. People gnawed their tongues because of their pain and blasphemed the God of heaven because of their pains and their sores, but they did not repent of their works (Revelation 16:10-11 CSB).

This fifth bowl will afflict the "throne of the beast." In other words, it will darken his kingdom. The beast—the final Antichrist—who had been granted some temporary authority over the earth, is seeing his short-lived kingdom coming to an inglorious end.

For the people still living upon the earth, the darkness would certainly increase their anxiety and fear. When this is combined with the horrible sores from the first bowl, it will make living on earth unbearable. Yet, the unbelievers, through all of this, still blaspheme God.

We will next look separately at two aspects of the judgment of the sixth bowl—the arrival of the Kings of the East and the gathering for the final battle—the campaign of Armageddon.

The Sixth Bowl Judgment: The Arrival of the Kings of the East, Armageddon (Revelation 16:13-16)

We now come to the judgment of the Lord associated with the "sixth bowl." The pouring out of this bowl will cause the Euphrates River to dry up, which will allow a massive troop movement of the "kings from the East" to gather together in preparation of a great battle—Armageddon. The Bible explains it in this manner

> The sixth angel poured out his bowl on the great river Euphrates, and its water was dried up to prepare the way for the kings from the East. Then I saw three impure spirits that looked like frogs; they came out of the mouth of the dragon, out of the mouth of the beast and out of the mouth of the false prophet. They are demonic spirits that perform signs, and they go out to the kings of the whole world, to gather them for the battle on the great day of God Almighty. "Look, I come like a thief! Blessed is the one who stays awake and remains clothed, so as not to go naked and be shamefully exposed." Then they gathered the kings together to the place that in Hebrew is called Armageddon (Revelation 16:13-15 NIV).

There are many things taking place here that need to be addressed.

First, we find that the Euphrates River will be dried up to prepare the way for these "kings from the East."

THE EUPHRATES RIVER IN SCRIPTURE

The Euphrates River, also called "the Great River," is prominent in Scripture. In fact, it is the northeastern border of the land God promised to Abraham's descendants:

> That day the Lord made a covenant with Abram: "To your descendants I give this land, from the river of Egypt to the great river, the Euphrates River" (Genesis 15:18 NET).

The Lord will dry up this river that had previously turned into blood.

GOD HAS LITERALLY DRIED UP RIVERS IN THE PAST

Some examples of God having literally worked in this way in the past are given to us in the Old Testament. The Bible relates the famous story of the Lord drying up the Red Sea so the Israelites could advance onto the Promised Land:

> Moses stretched his arm over the sea, and the Lord sent a strong east wind that blew all night until there was dry land where the water had been. The sea opened up, and the Israelites walked through on dry land with a wall of water on each side (Exodus 14:21-22 CEV).

In another episode, the Lord dried up the River Jordan so the Israelites could cross over to the Promised Land (Joshua 3:13-17, 4:23).

Elijah, the prophet, also parted the waters of the Jordan River:

> When they got there, Elijah took off his coat, then he rolled it up and struck the water with it. At once a path opened up through the river, and the two of them walked across on dry ground (2 Kings 2:8 CEV).

These Old Testament examples of the Lord drying up literal rivers, demonstrate that a literal fulfillment of this prophecy is what will take place. In other words, there is no need to see this "drying up" of the Euphrates River as something which is merely "symbolic."

THIS DRYING UP LEADS TO WAR

Something else to note is that this "drying up" of the river, in-and-of-itself, does not pose a problem for the people living at the time. It is the consequences of this event that becomes the problem. In other words, this act does not inflict some type of plague upon the people, but rather it sets the stage as a preparation for one of the great battles that is still to come, Armageddon.

THE FROGS

Following the drying up of the Euphrates River, we have the introduction of three unclean spirits that are said to be "like frogs." The fact that frogs are mentioned in this context should not be missed. We know that frogs were related to the Egyptian goddess Heqt during the time of Israel's bondage in Egypt. In response, the Lord sent a plague of frogs upon the land of Egypt (Exodus 8:1-6).

Therefore, the fact that they are mentioned in this context would cause the people to recall those horrific centuries of oppression, as well as the miraculous deliverance that the nation of Israel had experienced in the past. Again, we find a connection between the events in the Book of Revelation and the exodus from Egypt.

THOSE WHO REMAIN FAITHFUL WILL BE REWARDED

In the midst of this sixth bowl and the explanation of this coming war campaign, Armageddon, John records the following comforting words of the Lord:

> Look, I come like a thief! Blessed is the one who stays awake and remains clothed, so as not to go naked and be shamefully exposed (Revelation 16:15 NIV).

Recall that that this book was originally addressed by Jesus to the seven churches of Asia (Revelation 2:1–3:22). A major theme throughout Revelation is that the believers needed to persevere in the face of the difficult persecution that they were receiving. This same theme is now restated here. The Lord will indeed reward those believers who have been faithful to Him—those who remain clothed with His righteousness.

ARMAGEDDON

As the narrative continues, these "frog-like," evil spirits that we've mentioned, will bring together military units from all around the world to rally at a place called, in Hebrew, "Armageddon."

Armageddon is one of the most well-known words in the English language. Indeed, many people are aware that it speaks of some type of great battle or campaign that will take place at the "time of the end." However, there is much ignorance as to exactly what will happen at Armageddon. What does the Bible have to say about this coming event?

THE WORD IS FOUND IN ONLY ONE PLACE

For one thing, this particular word, "Armageddon," is found only in Revelation 16:16:

> So they assembled the kings at the place called in Hebrew, Armageddon (Revelation 16:16 CSB).

Simply put, Armageddon refers to the rallying-place of the kings of the earth, who, are led by these unclean spirits which come from the mouths of the evil, unholy trinity—the dragon, the beast, and the false prophet. They will muster their armies for the final war campaign against the Lord and His people, Israel.

THE MOUNTAIN OF MEGIDDO: THE SCENE OF PAST BATTLES

The word translated "Armageddon" is derived from Hebrew *har m'giddo*— the "mountain of Megiddo." The ancient Israelite town of

Megiddo guarded the pass of a main caravan route between the Plain of Sharon and the Valley of Jezreel. In other words, it has always been a strategic location.

In this context, Armageddon likely refers to the hill country surrounding the town of Megiddo which includes all the mountains that border the 14 by 20-mile Valley of Jezreel.

THE SCENE OF PAST BATTLES

The Valley of Jezreel, also called the Plain of Esdraelon, which is at the foot of Mount Megiddo, has been the scene of many significant battles in the history of the nation of Israel. They include: the victory of the Judge Deborah over Sisera (Judges 5:19-20), Gideon's defeat of the countless number of Midianites (Judges 6:33), the death of Saul at the hands of the army of the Philistines (1 Samuel 31, 2 Samuel 4:4), and the death of the good King Josiah in the unwise battle with Pharaoh Neco (2 Kings 23:29-30, 2 Chronicles 35:22).

In other words, in the long history of the nation of Israel, this location, the Mountain of Megiddo, has been the scene of many never-to-be-forgotten battles.

Therefore, it is poetic that this is the place where one of the last great battles between the Lord and the powers of evil will occur.

A PLACE WHERE THE ARMIES WILL ASSEMBLE

It has been noted that the plain of Megiddo, itself, is not large enough to contain armies from all over the world. Therefore, it should probably be understood as the staging area for a much larger military deployment. In fact, we are told that the battlefield will cover a two-hundred-mile distance!

We read about this slaughter that will take place, as well as the size of the battlefield, in a previous chapter:

Then the winepress was stomped outside the city, and blood poured out of the winepress up to the height of horses' bridles for a distance of almost two hundred miles (Revelation 14:20 NET).

IS ARMAGEDDON THE SAME BATTLE DESCRIBED IN EZEKIEL 38,39

There have been a number of commentators who believe that Ezekiel 38, 39 describe the Battle of Armageddon. However, a closer examination of these two events will demonstrate that they are not speaking of the same episode.

THE COMBATANTS ARE DIFFERENT

Ezekiel 38 names the specific combatants that will ally with one another to invade Israel. They are limited to seven or eight nations. On the other hand, Armageddon will involve all the nations of the earth.

ISRAEL IS NOT "AT PEACE" WHEN ARMAGEDDON HAPPENS

In Ezekiel, the Bible says that Israel will be "at rest" or "living securely" when they are invaded by these various nations.

On the other hand, the battle of Armageddon takes place at the end of the Great Tribulation period where the world is anything but "at peace" and "rest." Indeed, many from Israel will have fled into the wilderness to be supernaturally protected by the Lord. Other Jews will have been persecuted and killed.

THE ARMIES ARE DESTROYED IN DIFFERENT PLACES

We also find that in Ezekiel 39 the destruction of the various armies is upon the mountains of Israel. In contrast, there will be a two hundred mile stretch of land where the battle of Armageddon takes place.

THE ARMIES ARE DESTROYED BY DIFFERENT MEANS

Furthermore, in Ezekiel, the different armies are destroyed by various convulsions of nature which include hail, torrential downpours, fire and brimstone. However, at Armageddon they are destroyed by the personal appearance of Jesus Christ on His return to the earth.

Therefore, the battle of Revelation 16—Armageddon—is not the same as the invasion recorded in Ezekiel 38,39.

The King of the North and the King of the South
(Daniel 11:40-45)

In the Book of Daniel, we read of two kings who will do battle in the last days. They are known as the "king of the North" and "the king of the South." There has been much discussion as to their identities as well as how this war relates to two other major wars of the "last days"—the Ezekiel 38,39 invasion and the Battle of Armageddon.

Indeed, as we shall see, there are a number of scenarios which are proposed to describe this skirmish between the king of the North and the king of the South. Consequently, we will present several different viewpoints as to who these personages are, as well as how their fight relates to the invasion recorded in Ezekiel 38 and 39 and the famous Battle of Armageddon.

THE BACKGROUND: THE INTRODUCTION OF ANTIOCHUS IV

In Daniel 11:21-35 the subject is the eighth Seleucid-Greek ruler—Antiochus IV Epiphanes—who ruled from 175-163 B.C. He was introduced earlier as the "little horn" of Daniel (Daniel 8:9-12, 23-25).

Antiochus is highlighted in this section because of how his actions would affect the nation of Israel in a profound way. These predictions recorded in these verses have all been literally fulfilled in history.

THE PASSAGE MOVES TO THE TIME OF THE END (DANIEL 11:36-45)

While Daniel 11:21-35 chronicles Antiochus' evil deeds, the description moves from him to the personage of whom he is a "type"—the final Antichrist. While we have already given a general description of this coming evil individual (Event 9) these particular passages will add much to our knowledge.

As we look at the Scripture, it is the expression "the time of the end" (Daniel 11:35) which marks the sharp break in this prophecy. It's here that our focus is moved off of Antiochus, and onto a future "end times" personage. Up to this point, the prophecy in Daniel has been dealing with the Persian and Grecian Empires, which, as we look back, have been minutely fulfilled. Indeed, the precision is amazing!

Now, however, we are in an entirely different situation. In fact, every Bible commentator agrees that starting at Daniel 11:36, these passages have never been literally fulfilled in history, as have the other predictions recorded in this chapter of Daniel.

THIS HAS BEEN RECOGNIZED THROUGHOUT THE CENTURIES

Indeed, past students of the Scripture have recognized that another king, apart from Antiochus IV, must be in view in these passages of Daniel. These commentators include the fourth century writer Jerome, Martin Luther, as well as many others, who have identified this king with the final Antichrist—the last Gentile world ruler.

Daniel spoke of this time period as a time of distress:

> At that time Michael, the great prince who watches over your people, will arise. There will be a time of distress unlike any other from the nation's beginning up to that time (Daniel 12:1 NET).

This period—the "Great Tribulation"—is also referred to in the Book of Revelation:

Then one of the elders asked me, "These in white robes—
who are they, and where did they come from?" I answered,
"Sir, you know." And he said, "These are they who have come
out of the great tribulation; they have washed their robes
and made them white in the blood of the Lamb. (Revelation
7:13,14 NIV).

Furthermore, the time of "distress" or "tribulation" which is recorded
in Daniel 12:1 is the same future time period which Jesus spoke about:

For then there will be great tribulation, such as has not been
from the beginning of the world until now, no, and never
will be (Matthew 24:21 ESV).

This short period of time will occur immediately before the Lord
returns to the earth. Jesus also said:

Immediately after the tribulation of those days the sun will
be darkened, and the moon will not give its light, and the
stars will fall from heaven, and the powers of the heavens
will be shaken. Then will appear in heaven the sign of the
Son of Man, and then all the tribes of the earth will mourn,
and they will see the Son of Man coming on the clouds of
heaven with power and great glory. And he will send out his
angels with a loud trumpet call, and they will gather his elect
from the four winds, from one end of heaven to the other
(Matthew 24:29-31 ESV).

Indeed, by an examination of the Scriptures, we can know what is in
view by this "time of the end" spoken of in Daniel 11:35.

THE RESURRECTION OF THE OLD TESTAMENT BELIEVERS

Along with the examples that have already been given, there is further
evidence that the "Great Tribulation" becomes the subject in view here.
We have learned, so far, that this "coming king" will live in the "latter

days," and, when combined with what we read of in the following chapter of Daniel, chapter 12, we learn that this time is the same time when the resurrection of the Old Testament saints will take place. This resurrection will occur immediately *after* the Lord delivers His people from the power of this evil king—the final Antichrist. Daniel tells us the following:

> At that time shall arise Michael, the great prince who has charge of your people. And there shall be a time of trouble, such as never has been since there was a nation till that time. But at that time your people shall be delivered, everyone whose name shall be found written in the book. And many of those who sleep in the dust of the earth shall awake, some to everlasting life, and some to shame and everlasting contempt (Daniel 12:1,2 ESV).

Therefore, from all of the evidence, it is clear that this passage, along with Daniel 11:36 and following, is speaking of the latter part of the Great Tribulation period—the time of the end.

THE WILLFUL KING

Now, after the discussion of Antiochus (Daniel 11:21-35), Daniel introduces us to "the willful king:"

> And the king shall do as he wills. He shall exalt himself and magnify himself above every god, and shall speak astonishing things against the God of gods. He shall prosper till the indignation is accomplished; for what is decreed shall be done (Daniel 11:36 ESV).

As we noted, beginning in verse 36, Daniel describes events that have never been fulfilled in history. Indeed, Antiochus Epiphanes never desired to "exalt himself and magnify himself above every god."

Thus, the individual who is now in view is the future Antichrist who was first described in Daniel 7, and is also described in Chapter 9:

As I was contemplating the horns, another horn - a small one - came up between them, and three of the former horns were torn out by the roots to make room for it. This horn had eyes resembling human eyes and a mouth speaking arrogant things (Daniel 7:8 NET).

And after the sixty-two weeks, an anointed one shall be cut off and shall have nothing. And the people of the prince who is to come shall destroy the city and the sanctuary (Daniel 9:26 ESV).

Therefore, with these verses in mind, there would have been the expectation for the reader of Daniel to recognize this personage without the need for him to be re-introduced.

Consequently, many Bible students believe that this "willful king" is none other than the "little horn" of Daniel 7, as well as the "ruler" or "prince who is to come" of Daniel 9:26—the final Antichrist.

The New Testament calls this personage the "man of sin" or "the man of lawlessness:"

Let no one deceive you in any way. For that day will not come, unless the rebellion comes first, and the man of lawlessness is revealed, the son of destruction (2 Thessalonians 2:3 ESV).

ANTIOCHUS IS THE CLEAREST TYPE OF ANTICHRIST

In truth, a description of the final Antichrist should not be considered surprising in a context of describing Antiochus IV. In fact, Antiochus is the clearest type, or foreshadowing, of the coming Antichrist.

Consequently, Gabriel, at verse 36, has now ceased to speak of Antiochus and has begun to describe the final Antichrist of the last days. Daniel 11:37-39, therefore, provides us with a further description of this personage—the "willful king."

THE FUTURE WAR OF THE KING OF THE NORTH AND KING OF THE SOUTH

After the description of this king, who does according to his will, we now come to the account of the war the "king of the North" and the "king of the South" (Daniel 11:40-45). We must appreciate that when the Bible speaks of "north and south" it must be relative to the nation of Israel.

Earlier in Daniel Chapter 11, "the king of the South" represented the Egyptian leader while "the king of the North" described the Syrian king. As we mentioned, the battle described was fulfilled in the past, precisely as the Bible predicted.

Therefore, in this context, these kings of Daniel 11:40-45 must symbolize either nations, or confederations of nations, that will exist at the time of the end.

THERE ARE MANY QUESTIONS ABOUT THIS PASSAGE

While this passage relates a conflict between the "king of the North" and the "king of the South" in the last days, there are numerous issues that arise.

Two stand out: There is no consensus as to the identity of the "King of the North," neither is there any agreement as to the timing of this war.

ISSUE 1: WHO IS THE "KING OF THE NORTH?"

The identity of the king of the North is a matter of debate.

OPTION 1: THE KING OF THE NORTH IS THE FINAL ANTICHRIST

There is the view that this king of the North can be identified with the "willful king"—the final Antichrist—who has been the subject of verses 36-39. In this scenario, a king from the south will do battle against the Antichrist in the "last days."

Those who argue for two kings claim that it is much simpler to understand the "king of the North" in this verse to be none other than the latter-day "little horn" written about in the Book of Daniel—the final Antichrist.

Earlier in this chapter (Daniel 11:6-28) we find that a number of rulers from the Seleucid line were designated as "the king of the North." This includes Antiochus IV—who is the clearest type of the final Antichrist. Therefore, it would be consistent to designate both the type, as well as the literal fulfillment of the type, by the same phrase—"the king of the North."

Consequently, what we have in this context is a rebellion that breaks out against the worldwide rule of the Antichrist.

OPTION 2: THE KING OF THE NORTH IS NOT THE ANTICHRIST

On the other hand, some believe that this king of the North is distinct from the Antichrist. Therefore, we are dealing with three leaders—the king of the North, the king of the South, and the final Antichrist.

According to this scenario, both the king of the South and the king of the North, who are seemingly allies, will attack Antichrist on two fronts in the "last days."

There are several arguments that are offered that support this view.

First, in Daniel 11:36-39, the final Antichrist is simply called "the king." He is not designated as the "king of the North."

Second, Scripture says that the final Antichrist will arise from Rome. Rome is *not* directly north of the Holy Land. In the Bible, Babylon is described as being from the "north." For example, we read in Jeremiah:

> This is what the Lord says: 'Beware! An army is coming from a land in the north. A mighty nation is stirring into action in faraway parts of the earth. . . Listen! News is coming even now. The rumble of a great army is heard approaching from a land in the north. It is coming to turn the towns of Judah

into rubble, places where only jackals live (Jeremiah 6:22; 10:22 NET).

In addition, it is argued that the context favors this view of three kings, rather than two.

In sum, either view seems to be possible. This makes it difficult to come to a firm conclusion on the matter of the identity of the "king of the North." Our view is that there are only two kings and the "king of the North" is indeed the final Antichrist.

ISSUE 2: WHEN DOES THIS EVENT TAKE PLACE?

Not only are there questions with respect to the identity of the king of the North, the issue of the timing of the event is also in question. While it is agreed that it will take place in the "last days," there is no consensus as to how to relate it to the other coming wars mentioned in Scripture.

Some believe that this is the same invasion that is recorded in Ezekiel 38 and 39. Others argue that this event recorded here in Daniel is the Battle of Armageddon, while still others hold that this event describes both the Ezekiel invasion and Armageddon! In other words, the same event is described in three different portions of Scripture.

THIS IS NOT THE EZEKIEL 38,39 INVASION

For a number of reasons, it appears that this war recorded in Daniel is not the same event as recorded in Ezekiel 38,39.

THE TIMING IS DIFFERENT

The chronology of Daniel 11:36-39 refers to this latter period of world rule of the Antichrist, and, therefore, must occur after the Ezekiel 38,39 invasion, which seems to take place early in the final seven-year period.

Furthermore, when the Ezekiel invasion takes places, the people of Israel are seemingly lulled by a false security which will be guaranteed by this Final Antichrist. In fact, it is not until the mid-point of this last seven-year period that this man of sin turns on the people of Israel and attempts to destroy them.

GOG IS NOT THE ANTICHRIST

Also, the leader of the coalition in Ezekiel, Gog, is not the same personage as Antichrist. There are a number of reasons as to why this is so.

THEY LEAD DIFFERENT COALITIONS

First, the final Antichrist is the last Gentile "world ruler" while Gog is the leader of a regional "northern coalition" of nations that will invade Israel.

ANTICHRIST IS PART OF THE REVIVED ROMAN EMPIRE WHILE GOG IS FROM OUTSIDE THE EMPIRE

Second, the "little horn" in Daniel, the Antichrist, belongs to the Revived Roman Empire in its final form. Gog, however, comes from a region that is geographically from the far north. This area is outside of the boundaries of the ancient Roman Empire.

GOG MAKES NO COVENANT WITH THE JEWS AND DOES NOT KILL THE TWO WITNESSES

Lastly, Antichrist, the coming world leader, makes a covenant with the Jews which he also breaks. Furthermore, this man of sin kills the two witnesses that the Lord sends to Israel in the last days (Revelation 11). Scripture never says that Gog is involved in any of these events.

Therefore, we can conclude that the battle described in the eleventh chapter of Daniel is a later incident—likely taking place several years after the invasion described in Ezekiel.

Furthermore, the previous context indicates that this "willful king" is as an absolute ruler. This fits with other passages in the Bible which picture a worldwide government at the time of the end (Daniel 7:23, Revelation 13:7).

The war recorded here in Daniel is seemingly a rebellion against the global leadership of the final Antichrist. This world government, that will be in power, is going to be attacked.

In sum, none of these explanations of the identity of the king of the North, or the exact timing of this skirmish, can be proved beyond a reasonable doubt, for Daniel is not that specific as to the timing of the event. However, what it is clear is that this "willful king" will be opposed to Christ.

The Seventh Bowl Judgment: Worldwide Devastation (Revelation 16:17-21)

We now arrive at the last of the "bowl" judgments. With it, the judgments of the Lord will be finished. The Bible explains it in this manner:

> Finally the seventh angel poured out his bowl into the air and a loud voice came out of the temple from the throne, saying: "It is done!" Then there were flashes of lightning, roaring, and crashes of thunder, and there was a tremendous earthquake—an earthquake unequaled since humanity has been on the earth, so tremendous was that earthquake. The great city was split into three parts and the cities of the nations collapsed. So Babylon the great was remembered before God, and was given the cup filled with the wine made of God's furious wrath. Every island fled away and no mountains could be found. And gigantic hailstones, weighing about a hundred pounds each, fell from heaven on people, but they blasphemed God because of the plague of hail, since it was so horrendous (Revelation 16:17-21 NET).

JUDGMENT IS COMPLETE

The words "it is done," which are associated with the seventh bowl, indicate that there will be no more judgments once this one is completed. In other words, the coming kingdom of God is near at hand!

WHAT IS THE GREAT CITY?

We are told that an earthquake of unparalleled magnitude will shake the "great city," and divide it into three parts. What city is this?

OPTION 1: BABYLON

Some understand this to be Babylon. In fact, the words "the great" seems to support this view.

OPTION 2: ROME

There are a number of commentators who argue that this "great city" refers to Rome.

OPTION 3: JERUSALEM

Some understand this to be Jerusalem. There are a number of reasons given.

First, the exact words are used to describe Jerusalem earlier in Revelation:

> Their corpses will lie in the street of the great city that is symbolically called Sodom and Egypt, where their Lord was also crucified (Revelation 11:8 NET).

In addition, the topographical changes described in Zechariah 14:4 also fit what is recorded here:

> On that day his feet will stand on the Mount of Olives which lies to the east of Jerusalem, and the Mount of Olives will be split in half from east to west, leaving a great valley. Half the mountain will move northward and the other half southward (Zechariah 14:4 NET).

BABYLON IS DESTROYED

It seems that this unprecedented earthquake will essentially destroy all of the cities of the world. Included in this destruction will be the ancient city of Babylon on the Euphrates River. Babylon is the special object of God's judgment. Chapters 17 and 18 describe the fall of Babylon in more detail.

> In fact, the fall of Babylon is the main teaching with respect to the seventh bowl of judgment. As we have noted, it is an event that was announced earlier—Revelation 14:8—as well as being prefigured in Revelation 14:14-20.

THE TOPOGRAPHY OF THE EARTH WILL BE CHANGED

This devastating earthquake will also produce other effects. It will level mountains and cause islands to disappear. As the Flood of Noah produced global changes in the topography of the earth, so will this ruinous earthquake.

In fact, it will prepare the earth for the coming Eden-like conditions that the Old Testament prophets predicted. These perfect conditions will characterize the earth during the thousand-year reign of Jesus Christ upon the earth—the Millennium.

THE HAILSTONES

The Lord will also send huge hailstones as a punishment. These gigantic stones will crush many of the evil people who are still living upon the earth. We find in biblical history that hail was often used as God's instrument of divine judgment upon wicked people (Joshua 10:11, Job 38:22-23, Isaiah 28:2, Ezekiel 13:11-13).

THE HARD HEARTS OF THE PEOPLE

Tragically, the Bible tells us that these three series of divine judgments, the seals, the trumpets, and the bowls, will not cause the evil people of the world to repent of their sins and place their faith in Christ. On the contrary, like the Pharaoh of the Exodus, their hearts will continue to be hardened throughout all of these divine judgments.

Though the people of the earth are certainly not ignorant that the Lord Himself has sent all of these judgments, they will still continue to blaspheme His Holy name. This fact speaks volumes about the evil that is found in the human heart!

DO THESE BOWL JUDGMENTS TAKE PLACE BEFORE CHRIST RETURNS OR DURING HIS RETURN?

There is a debate as to whether these seven bowl judgments occur before Christ returns or during His return.

OPTION 1: THE JUDGMENTS TAKE PLACE DURING HIS RETURN

Some argue that the various bowl judgments take place during a specific forty-five-day period of time. This entire period of time, forty-five days, is also seen as the Second Coming of Christ. Those who hold this view appeal to the chronological note given in the Book of Daniel:

> And from the time that the regular burnt offering is taken away and the abomination that makes desolate is set up, there shall be 1,290 days. Blessed is he who waits and arrives at the 1,335 days (Daniel 12:11,12 ESV).

The second half of Daniel's seventieth week consists of one thousand two hundred and ninety days. This will bring us to the end of the Great Tribulation period. However, according to this passage, the blessings of the reign of Jesus Christ are not enjoyed until some forty-five days later—at one thousand three hundred and thirty-five days.

Therefore, it is contended that this forty-five-day period is the period in which these final bowl judgments, associated with the Second Coming of Christ, are poured out on the earth. Consequently, that final forty-five-day period could rightly be called the Second Coming of Christ.

In this case, the one thousand two hundred and ninety days come to their completion with the appearance of the sign of the Son of Man in heaven (Matthew 24:30). After this, the judgments of Revelation 16 will follow in a forty-five-day period which will be concluded with the literal, physical descent of Christ to the earth.

OPTION 2: PREPARATION FOR THE MILLENNIUM

Another view is that the forty-five day period is the time of preparation for the beginning of the Millennium which will follow the Second Coming of Christ. Those who hold this view say it is wrong to describe the return of the Lord as taking place over a forty-five-day period. Indeed, it does not fit with what was said when the Lord left this world:

> After he had said this, while they were watching, he was lifted up and a cloud hid him from their sight. As they were still staring into the sky while he was going, suddenly two men in white clothing stood near them and said, "Men of Galilee, why do you stand here looking up into the sky? This same Jesus who has been taken up from you into heaven will come back in the same way you saw him go into heaven" (Acts 1:9-11 NET).

When Christ returns, it will be in the same manner, as well as at the same place where He left this world—at the Mount of Olives.

The bowl judgments, therefore, describe what happens *before* Jesus Christ returns, rather than during His return. These judgments then set the stage for the return of the Lord to the earth. This seems to be the best way to understand what is to come.

The Destruction of Damascus
(Isaiah 17:1, Jeremiah 49:23-27)

Isaiah 17, as well as Jeremiah 49, record prophecies concerning the future of the city of Damascus. We will look at each of these predictions as we attempt to understand why there are some Bible interpreters who believe these passages refer to an event that will take place at the time of the end.

ISAIAH AND DAMASCUS

Isaiah wrote the following about the fate of Damascus:

> A prophecy against Damascus: "See, Damascus will no longer be a city but will become a heap of ruins. The cities of Aroer will be deserted and left to flocks, which will lie down, with no one to make them afraid. The fortified city will disappear from Ephraim, and royal power from Damascus; the remnant of Aram will be like the glory of the Israelites," declares the Lord Almighty (Isaiah 17:1-3 NIV).

How are we to understand this prediction?

OPTION 1: THIS HAS ALREADY BEEN FULFILLED IN THE DISTANT PAST

Many commentators believe that this passage in Isaiah did speak of the future, but not of the distant future. They contend that it was literally fulfilled soon after the time Isaiah gave the prophecy. That literal fulfillment, with respect to Damascus, took place around 732 B.C.

For one thing, this prophecy dealt not only with Damascus, but also with the cities of Syria, as well as with Samaria—the capital of the northern kingdom of Israel. Consequently, the prophecy dealt with Israel as well as Syria and its cities some seven hundred years before the time of Christ.

According to the prophecy of Isaiah, each city would soon fall. Indeed, the Assyrians destroyed Damascus in 732 B.C., and Samaria some ten years later in 722 B.C.

As the Bible predicted, these cities became grazing lands with only a few people left in them. Therefore, we are dealing with predictions that have been literally fulfilled in the distant past.

OPTION 2: THE PREDICTION HAS YET TO BE FULFILLED

While there has been a past fulfilment for this passage, some commentators believe that what took place in 732 B.C. does not exhaust the prediction. In other words, this is also a prediction of a specific future event—the final destruction of Damascus. Indeed, there has never been the literal destruction of the city as found in this prediction—it has never become an "ash heap."

Support for this viewpoint is the fact that Isaiah repeats the phrase "in that day" in the context (verses 4, 7, 9, 11). This seems to point to a fulfillment of this prophecy at the "end of days." With that said, the Assyrian conquest of Damascus would be a foreshadowing of a much more serious conquest in the "last days."

While this argument has convinced a number of people that there is a future predicted destruction of Damascus, there are many good Bible prophecy specialists that deny that this is what is taught in this passage. They believe this prediction was fulfilled with the Assyrian conquest in 732 B.C.

THE PROPHECY IN JEREMIAH CONCERNING DAMASCUS

Jeremiah also wrote about Damascus some one hundred years after the time of Isaiah:

The Lord spoke about Damascus. "The people of Hamath and Arpad will be dismayed because they have heard bad news. Their courage will melt away because of worry. Their hearts will not be able to rest. The people of Damascus will lose heart and turn to flee. Panic will grip them.

> Pain and anguish will seize them like a woman in labor. How deserted will that once-famous city be, that city that was once filled with joy! For her young men will fall in her city squares. All her soldiers will be destroyed at that time," says the Lord who rules over all. "I will set fire to the walls of Damascus; it will burn up the palaces of Ben Hadad" (Jeremiah 49:23-27 NET).

This is another prediction about the fate of Damascus. While Isaiah was writing about the judgment upon the northern kingdom of Israel, Jeremiah is addressing the southern kingdom of Judah which went into captivity in 606 B.C.

Recall, it was the Assyrians who took the northern kingdom of Israel into captivity in 722 B.C. The Lord, through Jeremiah, is now predicting that those who took Israel captive would themselves be taken captive by the Babylonians. In sum, this prediction concerns the nation that conquered both Israel and Damascus at that time—Assyria.

This prediction of Jeremiah was literally fulfilled when Babylon conquered Assyria. The people of Damascus, controlled by the Assyrians, were also carried away into exile in 606 B.C.

THE CITY OF DAMASCUS REMAINS

The city of Damascus has not been once-and-for all destroyed. In fact, it remains one of the oldest continuous existing cities in the world. Does this mean that there is still a future destruction where it will be turned into an "ash heap," as Isaiah 17:1 predicts? Good Bible students hold various views.

WILL THE CITY BE DESTROYED IN "A DAY?"

There is a passage found in this same chapter in Isaiah that has been used to support the idea of a future destruction of Damascus. It reads as follows:

> At evening time, behold, terror! Before morning, they are no more! This is the portion of those who loot us, and the lot of those who plunder us (Isaiah 17:14 ESV).

While this passage is often used to claim that Damascus will be destroyed in "a day," it does nothing of the sort. To begin with, the context is not referring merely to the city of Damascus. In fact, it is speaking of many nations which will descend upon Israel like the waves of the sea. The Lord warns these nations that they would quickly dissipate because He Himself would punish them. Indeed, we are told that they would disappear like dust before a strong wind. Putting it another way, the terror they would bring at night would vanish by the next day.

The fact that Isaiah does not mention a particular nation as the enemy, indicates that it is not merely one particular nation that is in view here. In fact, it is a repetition of what the Lord promised to Abraham and his descendants:

> I will bless those who bless you, and whoever curses you I will curse (Genesis 12:3 NIV).

Therefore, neither this passage, or any other in Scripture, predicts that the city of Damascus will be destroyed in "a day."

THE TIMING OF ANY FULFILLMENT IS UNCERTAIN

As mentioned, there are those who believe that a future destruction of Damascus is still to be fulfilled. Even if this is true, there is no certainty as to the timing.

Some argue that it will take place before the Great Tribulation period, others at the very beginning of the period, while still others argue it will take place later in this final seven-year period. In other words, the precise timing is not known.

Therefore, if indeed these two passages are a prediction of the final future destruction of this ancient city, how and when it fits into the "last days" scenario is unclear. However, as we also indicated, there are a number of prophecy specialists who do not see any prediction in Scripture of a future destruction of Damascus.

The Conversion of Egypt
(Isaiah 19:18, 19)

One of the most amazing predictions in Scripture concerns Israel's historical enemy—Egypt. The passage reads as follows:

> At that time five cities in the land of Egypt will speak the language of Canaan and swear allegiance to the Lord who commands armies. One will be called the City of the Sun. At that time there will be an altar for the Lord in the middle of the land of Egypt, as well as a sacred pillar dedicated to the Lord at its border (Isaiah 19:18,19 NET).

The Egyptians will one day turn in faith to the God of Abraham, Isaac, and Jacob!

THE TIME IS STILL FUTURE

We find four different statements in this context, each introduced by the phrase "in that day." They are as follows:

> In that day the Egyptians will be like women, and tremble with fear before the hand that the Lord of hosts shakes over them. . . . In that day there will be five cities in the land of Egypt that speak the language of Canaan and swear allegiance to the Lord of hosts. . . . In that day there will be an altar to the Lord in the midst of the land of Egypt, and

> a pillar to the Lord at its border. It will be a sign and a wit-
> ness to the Lord of hosts in the land of Egypt. . . . And
> the Lord will make himself known to the Egyptians, and the
> Egyptians will know the Lord in that day and worship with
> sacrifice and offering, and they will make vows to the Lord
> and perform them (Isaiah 19:16,18,19, 23 ESV).

This phrase, "in that day," is used almost always in Scripture to refer to the time of the end. Furthermore, it does not refer to some specific twenty-four-hour period, but to a more general time in the future. A good English equivalent is "at that time."

Therefore, at a particular time in the future, a series of events will take place that will forever change the situation of the people of Egypt. Indeed, those in Egypt will turn from being antagonistic to the Lord, to putting their trust in Him.

THREE MONUMENTAL THINGS WILL HAPPEN

Scripture speaks of three events that will take place.

First, there will be several Egyptian cities that will speak Hebrew, "the language of Canaan," as well as swear allegiance to the Lord (Isaiah 19:18). In fact, it seems that one of these five cities will actually be the home city of the cult of the sun god—Re!

> Next, we are told that the Lord, the God of Israel, will be
> worshiped in Egypt with an "altar" in the center of the land,
> as well as with a "monument" on their border (Isaiah 19:19).

It is likely, that there is not merely one altar and one memorial. Instead, this "altar" and "memorial" may represent many worship centers. If this is the case, then it would be similar to what the Bible said of Abraham and Jacob. These two patriarchs built altars and memorial pillars in vari-ous places in the Promised Land (Genesis 12:8, 28:18). In doing so, they acknowledged the presence of the Lord in their lives wherever they went.

EGYPT AND ASSYRIA WILL WORSHIP THE LORD

We also discover that the Lord is not only going to deliver Egypt and Israel from the oppression of the Assyrians, but these three countries will eventually be joined together in common worship of the Lord. Specifically, Egypt and Assyria will travel back and forth to each other's countries to worship the God of Abraham, Isaac, and Jacob. In fact, the Lord calls Egypt "my people" and Assyria "the work of My hands:"

> Whom the Lord of hosts has blessed, saying, "Blessed be Egypt my people, and Assyria the work of my hands, and Israel my inheritance" (Isaiah 19:25 ESV).

Therefore, a glorious future awaits Egypt and Assyria.

The Final Siege and Deliverance of Jerusalem (Zechariah 12-14)

Jerusalem is the one city in the world where the Lord has placed His holy name. Indeed, according to Scripture, more than any city on our planet, God's program revolves around this holy city. At the time of the end, connected with the Battle of Armageddon, there will be a final attempt to once-and-for-all destroy Jerusalem and its inhabitants.

THE LORD GATHERS ALL NATIONS AGAINST JERUSALEM

Zechariah the prophet records that the Lord will gather all the nations of the earth for a last battle against Jerusalem. We read:

> A prophecy: The word of the LORD concerning Israel. The LORD, who stretches out the heavens, who lays the foundation of the earth, and who forms the spirit in human beings, declares: I am going to make Jerusalem a cup that sends all the surrounding peoples reeling. Judah will be besieged as well as Jerusalem. On that day, when all the nations of the earth are gathered against her, I will make Jerusalem an immovable rock for all the nations. All who try to move it will injure themselves (Zechariah 12:1-3 NIV).

There are a number of things that we learn from this passage. They include the following:

After the introduction, we learn that the deliverance of Jerusalem will come at the time of the end, "on that day." In fact, all nations are gathered against Jerusalem in this final conflict—the War, or Campaign, of Armageddon.

Described in Revelation 16:13-16, we are told that the nations will gather in the Jezreel Valley, in front of Mt. Megiddo, and will then make their way to the city of Jerusalem. Scripture says:

> And they assembled them at the place that in Hebrew is called Armageddon (Revelation 16:16 ESV).

At Megiddo, the troops will muster for this march to Jerusalem.

However, their attempt to destroy the holy city will cause them to be destroyed. Indeed, the Lord has promised that Jerusalem will be a cup that causes "reeling" and be an "immovable rock" for these nations. The imagery is that Jerusalem will be a cup of wine that will make the nations stagger in drunkenness. The psalmist used this same illustration:

> You have shown your people desperate times; you have given us wine that makes us stagger (Psalm 60:3 NIV).

Jerusalem is also likened to an immovable rock that is so heavy that it will cause injury to the nations that try to lift it.

THE LORD WILL SUPERNATURALLY LIBERATE JERUSALEM

In response to the siege of the nations, the Lord will liberate Jerusalem through divine disruption of these attacking armies. We are told that God will strike every horse and rider with madness and blindness:

> On that day I will strike every horse with panic and its rider with madness," declares the Lord. "I will keep a watchful eye over Judah, but I will blind all the horses of the nations. Then the clans of Judah will say in their hearts, 'The people of Jerusalem are strong, because the Lord Almighty is their God' (Zechariah 12:4-5 NIV).

The inhabitants of the city will realize that the Lord is on their side.

Jerusalem, the "holy city," will not be destroyed:

> On that day I will make the clans of Judah like a firepot in a woodpile, like a flaming torch among sheaves. They will consume all the surrounding peoples right and left, but Jerusalem will remain intact in her place (Zechariah 12:6 NIV).

Though surrounded and hopelessly outnumbered, the entire city will remain intact:

> On that day the Lord will shield those who live in Jerusalem, so that the feeblest among them will be like David, and the house of David will be like God, like the angel of the Lord going before them. On that day I will set out to destroy all the nations that attack Jerusalem (Zechariah 12:8-9 NIV).

God's intervention on the side of Israel will result in a divine slaughter of all the armies of the nations that come against Jerusalem. The Bible emphasizes that though Israel will fight powerfully, its strength and success will actually come from the Lord God—the God of Abraham, Isaac, and Jacob.

Later in the Book of Zechariah, we read about this conflict. It says:

> A day of the LORD is coming, Jerusalem, when your possessions will be plundered and divided up within your very walls. I will gather all the nations to Jerusalem to fight against it; the city will be captured, the houses ransacked, and the women ravished. Half of the city will go into exile, but the rest of the people will not be taken from the city. Then the LORD will go out and fight against those nations, as he fights on a day of battle (Zechariah 14:1-3 NIV).

Though all seems to be lost, one last time, the Lord will supernaturally intervene and rescue Jerusalem from its enemies.

The National Conversion of Israel and Great Promise for Their Future (Zechariah 14)

The Jewish nation, as well as its leadership, rejected the Messiah—Jesus of Nazareth—during His First Coming to the earth. As a result of their rejection, Christ pronounced judgment upon them. Within a generation Jerusalem and the temple were destroyed, and the people were sent into exile.

However, the Lord also gave a message of hope to the "chosen" people. The Bible says that at the time of the end, the people of Israel, as a nation, will turn to Jesus, their Messiah, for forgiveness. When this occurs, He will return to the earth.

THERE WILL BE A TIME OF REPENTANCE FOR ISRAEL

As we saw in our previous event, there will be a final siege of Jerusalem in the "last days." This siege, or campaign of Armageddon, will take place immediately before the coming of the Lord.

At the climax of the campaign of Armageddon, when Israel's enemies are ransacking Jerusalem, Israel will turn to the Messiah Jesus in mourning. They will call for His deliverance.

Scripture says that after the physical deliverance from their enemies, (Zechariah 12:1-9), the nation of Israel will experience a spiritual deliverance (Zechariah 12:10-14). The Bible explains it this way:

> And I will pour out on the house of David and the inhabitants of Jerusalem a spirit of grace and supplication. They will look on me, the one they have pierced, and they will mourn for him as one mourns for an only child, and grieve bitterly for him as one grieves for a firstborn son. On that day the weeping in Jerusalem will be as great as the weeping of Hadad Rimmon in the plain of Megiddo. The land will mourn, each clan by itself, with their wives by themselves: the clan of the house of David and their wives, the clan of the house of Nathan and their wives, the clan of the house of Levi and their wives, the clan of Shimei and their wives, and all the rest of the clans and their wives (Zechariah 12:10-14 NIV).

It is at this time, when the Lord delivers them from their physical enemies, that they will recognize Jesus as their Messiah. As a result, the people will weep and mourn.

ZECHARIAH 14: THE DAY OF THE LORD: WHEN EVENING TURNS INTO MORNING

At the time of Israel's repentance, the "dark evening" of the "day of the Lord" will be coming to a close, with a new day about to dawn. As we saw in a previous event (Event 4), the day of the Lord is a period of time when the Lord will pour out His judgment upon a Christ-rejecting world, followed by His return where He judges sin and then rules in righteousness. We can compare this time period to a dark evening, when judgment comes, and then the dawn of the morning, when the Lord appears.

Zechariah 14 provides us with an example where the dark evening portion of the "day of the Lord" turns into the bright morning with the mighty deliverance of the Lord.

It is here that we will also read of God's mighty faithfulness to His chosen nation, Israel, and His great promises for their future.

FROM EVENING TO DAWN: THE PROMISES OF ISRAEL'S FUTURE

First, the future devastation of Jerusalem is predicted. This will be a dark time when all the nations of the world will gather against this holy city. Their enemies will capture part of Jerusalem, plunder the houses of the Jews, rape the Jewish women, and then exile half of those who survive. The Lord said:

> For I will gather all the nations against Jerusalem to wage war; the city will be taken, its houses plundered, and the women raped. Then half of the city will go into exile, but the remainder of the people will not be taken away (Zechariah 14:2 NET).

However, in the midst of this crisis, the Lord will declare His own sovereign control over these horrific events. As terrible as these things will be, the nation of Israel must remember that it is the Lord who will ultimately bring about their deliverance. In fact, after Zechariah describes the future devastation of Jerusalem, he then predicts their future deliverance (14:3-21). Included are seven distinct promises from the Lord. They include the following:

PROMISE 1: THE LORD WILL RESCUE HIS PEOPLE

First, God promises to rescue the Jewish people from this terrible conflict in Jerusalem:

> Then the Lord will go to battle and fight against those nations, just as he fought battles in ancient days. On that day his feet will stand on the Mount of Olives which lies to the east of Jerusalem, and the Mount of Olives will be split in half from east to west, leaving a great valley. Half the mountain will move northward and the other half southward. Then you will escape through my mountain valley, for the mountains will extend to Azal. Indeed, you will flee as you fled from the earthquake in the days of King Uzziah of

Judah. Then the Lord my God will come with all his holy ones with him (Zechariah 14:3-5 NET).

In response to the national repentance of Israel, as well as their turning in faith to Jesus the Messiah, the Lord declares that He will fight against those nations who have attacked the "holy city." In fact, He will end the siege by Jesus' physical return to the Mount of Olives.

This will fulfill the promise given to His disciples as the Lord was ascending into heaven:

> After he [Jesus] said this, he was taken up before their very eyes, and a cloud hid him from their sight: They were looking intently up into the sky as he was going, when suddenly two men dressed in white stood beside them. "Men of Galilee," they said, "why do you stand here looking into the sky? This same Jesus, who has been taken from you into heaven, will come back in the same way you have seen him go into heaven" (Acts 1:9-11 NIV).

Not only will Jesus physically return to the Mount of Olives, we are also told that this mountain will split from east to west and provide a way of escape for those who are trapped in Jerusalem.

PROMISE 2: THE LORD WILL REMAKE THE AREAS AROUND JERUSALEM

The Lord then promised to give some supernatural signs in the heavens as well as make some physical changes around the city of Jerusalem:

> On that day there will be no light-the sources of light in the heavens will congeal. It will happen in one day (a day known to the Lord); not in the day or the night, but in the evening there will be light. Moreover, on that day living waters will flow out from Jerusalem, half of them to the eastern sea and half of them to the western sea; it will happen both in summer and in winter (Zechariah 14:6-8 NET).

There will be supernatural signs in the sky which includes an evening where there will be light.

In addition, there will be a river of living water flowing out of Jerusalem to the eastern sea, the Dead Sea, as well as to the western sea, the Mediterranean Sea. Thus, the entire land of Israel will be irrigated year-round. Droughts, therefore, will be a thing of the past.

> The prophet Ezekiel also predicted that the Dead Sea would be revitalized during the time of the reign of the Messiah (Ezekiel 47:8-12).

PROMISE 3: THE LORD WILL REIGN FROM JERUSALEM

We then have the promise that the Lord, Jesus the Messiah, will rule from Jerusalem:

> The Lord will then be king over all the earth. In that day the Lord will be seen as one with a single name (Zechariah 14:9 NET).

The Lord will rule over the entire world with Jerusalem as His capital.

PROMISE 4: THE LORD WILL RENOVATE THE TOPOGRAPHY OF JERUSALEM

Jerusalem itself will see a geographical change:

> All the land will change and become like the Arabah from Geba to Rimmon, south of Jerusalem; and Jerusalem will be raised up and will stay in its own place from the Benjamin Gate to the site of the First Gate and on to the Corner Gate, and from the Tower of Hananel to the royal winepresses. And people will settle there, and there will no longer be the threat of divine extermination-Jerusalem will dwell in security (Zechariah 14:10-11 NET).

The topography of the city will be changed. The land around Jerusalem, both to the north, Geba, as well as to the south, Rimmon, will be flattened. In contrast, Jerusalem itself will be elevated. With this change, Israel will dwell in complete security.

PROMISE 5: THE LORD WILL PUNISH THOSE WHO OPPRESS JERUSALEM

Those who fought against Jerusalem will be punished:

> But this will be the nature of the plague with which the Lord will strike all the nations that have fought against Jerusalem: Their flesh will decay while they stand on their feet, their eyes will rot away in their sockets, and their tongues will dissolve in their mouths. On that day there will be great confusion from the Lord among them; they will seize each other and attack one another violently. Moreover, Judah will fight at Jerusalem, and the wealth of all the surrounding nations will be gathered up-gold, silver, and clothing in great abundance. This is the kind of plague that will devastate horses, mules, camels, donkeys, and all the other animals in those camps (Zechariah 14:12-15 NET).

The Lord then promised to punish those who oppressed of Jerusalem with judgments of both plague and panic. In addition, their wealth will now go to the people of Judah. All of this will take place at the culmination of the battle of Armageddon.

PROMISE 6: THE LORD WILL ESTABLISH UNIVERSAL WORSHIP IN JERUSALEM

Next, we find that universal worship of the Lord will be the new rule:

> Then all who survive from all the nations that came to attack Jerusalem will go up annually to worship the King, the Lord who rules over all, and to observe the Feast of Tabernacles. But if any of the nations anywhere on earth refuse to go up to Jerusalem to worship the King, the Lord who rules over all, they will get no rain. If the Egyptians will not do so, they

will get no rain - instead there will be the kind of plague which the Lord inflicts on any nations that do not go up to celebrate the Feast of Tabernacles. This will be the punishment of Egypt and of all nations that do not go up to celebrate the Feast of Tabernacles (Zechariah 14:16-19 NET).

Scripture tells us that a large number of Gentiles will embrace Jesus as their Savior during the Great Tribulation period. Many will survive this difficult period. These believers in Christ, the tribulation saints, will go up each year to Jerusalem to worship the King, Jesus.

They will also celebrate the Feast of Booths, or Tabernacles. This will be a required festival of the earthly kingdom of Jesus.

PROMISE 7: JERUSALEM SHALL BE A COMPLETELY "HOLY CITY"

This last promise concerns Jerusalem. The city will become one of "complete holiness:"

> On that day the bells of the horses will bear the inscription "Holy to the Lord." The cooking pots in the Lord's temple will be as holy as the bowls in front of the altar. Every cooking pot in Jerusalem and Judah will become holy in the sight of the Lord who rules over all, so that all who offer sacrifices may come and use some of them to boil their sacrifices in them. On that day there will no longer be a Canaanite in the house of the Lord who rules over all (Zechariah 14:20,21 NET).

Jerusalem will indeed be the "holy city." In other words, it will be set apart from everything that is unholy. Of the utmost importance, all people who worship the King will be holy.

These are some of the wonderful promises of God for the descendants of Abraham, Isaac, and Jacob as well as for the holy city of Jerusalem.

EVENT 32

The Banquet at the Wedding Celebration of the Lamb (Revelation 19:6-9)

The Bible speaks of a future event known as the "marriage supper of the Lamb," or better yet, the "banquet at the wedding celebration of the Lamb." We read about this in the Book of Revelation:

> Then I heard what sounded like the voice of a vast throng, like the roar of many waters and like loud crashes of thunder. They were shouting: "Hallelujah! For the Lord our God, the All-Powerful, reigns! Let us rejoice and exult and give him glory, because the wedding celebration of the Lamb has come, and his bride has made herself ready. She was permitted to be dressed in bright, clean, fine linen" (for the fine linen is the righteous deeds of the saints). Then the angel said to me, "Write the following: Blessed are those who are invited to the banquet at the wedding celebration of the Lamb!" He also said to me, "These are the true words of God" (Revelation 19:6-9 NET).

Simply put, the "banquet at the wedding celebration of the Lamb" is a future celebration of the Lord with His people.

This definition brings up a number of questions. Who are the participants? When will this event take place? How long will this celebration last? What does the Bible say about this coming event?

BOTH TESTAMENTS LOOK FORWARD TO THIS EVENT

In the Old Testament, we find the Lord is symbolically portrayed as the husband of Israel:

> For your husband is the one who made you-the Lord who commands armies is his name. He is your protector, the Holy One of Israel. He is called "God of the entire earth" (Isaiah 54:5 NIV).

As such, He promised Israel, His wife, that a lavish banquet awaited her, as well as believing Gentiles, at a future time:

In Jerusalem, the Lord of Heaven's Armies will spread a wonderful feast

> for all the people of the world. It will be a delicious banquet with clear, well-aged wine and choice meat. There he will remove the cloud of gloom, the shadow of death that hangs over the earth. He will swallow up death forever! The Sovereign Lord will wipe away all tears. He will remove forever all insults and mockery against his land and people. The Lord has spoken! (Isaiah 25:6-8 NLT).

Along with the description of this banquet, we find that death will be destroyed and all tears wiped away!

JESUS PROMISED THE SAME BANQUET FOR BELIEVERS

We also find the Lord Jesus, on a number of occasions, promising a similar banquet to those who believe in Him. They are as follows:

THE HEALING OF THE CENTURION'S SERVANT

After Jesus healed a servant of a certain centurion, He spoke about Gentiles feasting with Abraham, Isaac, and Jacob in His future kingdom:

> I tell you, many will come from the east and west to share the banquet with Abraham, Isaac, and Jacob in the kingdom of heaven (Matthew 8:11 NET).

This is consistent with what the Lord said in Isaiah. Gentiles, as well as Jews, will participate in this coming feast.

THE PARABLE OF THE WEDDING BANQUET

On two occasions, it is recorded that Jesus gave the parable of the wedding banquet (Matthew 22:1–14, Luke 14:16–24). In this parable, the Lord pronounced judgment on the Jewish religious leaders of his day. These are the ones who rejected his invitation to become part of His kingdom.

On the other hand, the Lord then announced that the unworthy would attend the banquet instead of them. These attendees, who placed their faith in Him, would consist of the so-called "sinners" of Israel as well as the despised heathens, the Gentiles.

THE PARABLE OF THE TEN MAIDENS IS LINKED TO THE TIME OF THE END

The Lord also highlighted this future wedding feast in the parable of the ten virgins, or the ten maidens (Matthew 25:1–13). From this parable, we find that only those who are ready and prepared for the coming of the groom, Jesus, will accompany Him to this future wedding feast.

Furthermore, in this context, we also find that Jesus explicitly connects this "wedding banquet" with events that will follow His unexpected Second Coming to the earth. In fact, He gave this ominous warning:

> Therefore stay alert, because you do not know the day or the hour (Matthew 25:13 NET).

On another occasion, He said:

> You also must be ready, because the Son of Man will come at an hour when you do not expect him (Luke 12:40 NET).

Therefore, the idea of a future wedding banquet, with the Lord and His people, is something that is taught in both testaments.

THE BANQUET REVEALS THE INTIMATE NATURE BETWEEN THE LORD AND THE BELIEVERS

The promise of this future wedding banquet between the Lord and His people emphasizes the personal and intimate relationship which believers experience with Him.

Indeed, in biblical times, meals were occasions for close, personal fellowship. The Bible gives a number of examples of this.

We find that Jesus promised to the church at Laodicea that He would "share a meal with them" if they repented from their actions:

> Listen! I am standing at the door and knocking! If anyone hears my voice and opens the door I will come into his home and share a meal with him, and he with me (Revelation 3:20 NET).

Those who open the door of their heart to Christ will experience this intimate fellowship with Him.

> The Lord's Supper is another example of this personal type of fellowship. In fact, the celebration of the Lord's Supper becomes a preview of the eternal fellowship that believers will experience with their Lord (1 Corinthians 11:17–34).

All in all, this marriage banquet portrays a time of celebration and intimate fellowship with the King.

THE TIMING OF THE EVENT

Bible believers have different views as to the exact timing of this event. The suggestions are as follows:

OPTION 1: ON EARTH AT THE BEGINNING OF THE MILLENNIUM

This first option holds that it will take place on earth at the beginning of the Millennium—at the time of Christ's return. In other words, at His return all believers will participate in this wedding banquet.

OPTION 2: THROUGHOUT THE MILLENNIUM

There is also the opinion that this feast continues throughout the thousand- year-period and concludes at the end of the Millennium.

OPTION 3: AT THE BEGINNING OF MILLENNIUM AND CONTINUING THROUGHOUT ETERNITY

There is also the view that this feast continues throughout all eternity.

Since the Scripture is silent as to the timing and duration of this future feast, we cannot answer these questions with certainty.

THE CONTRAST BETWEEN THE TWO BANQUETS

There is another banquet that we've yet to mention, the "great banquet of God." The marriage banquet of the Lamb stands in complete contrast to the "great banquet of God." This is the event where the Lord destroys His enemies at His coming and the birds consume their dead bodies:

> Then I saw an angel standing in the sun, shouting to the vultures flying high in the sky: "Come! Gather together for the great banquet God has prepared. Come and eat the flesh of kings, generals, and strong warriors; of horses and their riders; and of all humanity, both free and slave, small and great" . . . Their entire army was killed by the sharp sword that came from the mouth of the one riding the white horse. And the vultures all gorged themselves on the dead bodies (Revelation 19:17–18, 21 NLT).

Ironically, while the people of God will revel in this wonderful banquet of the Lamb, the evil people, who have rejected the message of Jesus Christ, will themselves be the banquet for the birds of prey!

This sums up some of the main points which the Bible makes about the coming "wedding banquet of the Lamb." What a wonderful time it will be!

The Sign of the Son of Man
(Matthew 24:30)

When asked about His coming back to the earth, the Lord Jesus pointed to the "sign of the Son of Man." The Bible records what He said as follows:

> Immediately after the distress of those days the sun will be darkened, and the moon will not give its light; the stars will fall from the sky, and the heavenly bodies will be shaken. Then will appear the sign of the Son of Man in heaven. And then all the peoples of the earth will mourn when they see the Son of Man coming on the clouds of heaven, with power and great glory (Matthew 24:29-30 NIV).

What exactly was He referring to? What precisely is the "sign of the Son of Man?"

THIS IS A SIGN OF THE SECOND COMING OF CHRIST

To begin with, we must understand that this is a sign of His Second Coming to the earth, it is not a sign of the rapture of the church. The Bible explains His return in this manner:

> Look, he is coming with the clouds," and "every eye will see him, even those who pierced him"; and all peoples on earth "will mourn because of him." So shall it be! Amen (Revelation 1:7 NIV).

Therefore, this particular sign has to do with His physical return to the earth.

THE VARIOUS VIEWS OF THE "SIGN"

So, what is *the* sign? Among Bible-believers there is debate as to whether this specific "sign" is some sort of heavenly ensign, or banner, that is seen when Christ appears, or whether the sign is actually Christ Himself.

OPTION 1: THE ENSIGN OR BANNER

The Greek word that is translated as "sign" could also be rendered "ensign," "standard," or "flag." This may have some Old Testament connections with the blowing of the shofar, the ram's horn.

THE BLOWING OF THE TRUMPET

In this context of our Lord speaking of His Second Coming, we find that the blowing of the trumpet will take place:

> And he will send out his angels with the mighty blast of a trumpet, and they will gather his chosen ones from all over the world—from the farthest ends of the earth and heaven (Matthew 24:31 NLT).

When the trumpet, the shofar, was blown in ancient Israel, a banner with a crosspiece at the top was raised. An animal, usually a snake, was affixed to the banner.

THE ENEMIES OF ISRAEL ARE ABOUT TO BE CRUSHED

This idea of a banner, or signal flag, is found in the writings of the prophet Isaiah, where it is connected to the "last days." We find, there, that at the "time of the end" the Lord will raise His banner as He is about to destroy the enemies of Israel:

At that time a root from Jesse will stand like a signal flag for the nations. Nations will look to him for guidance, and his residence will be majestic. At that time the sovereign master will again lift his hand to reclaim the remnant of his people from Assyria, Egypt, Pathros, Cush, Elam, Shinar, Hamath, and the seacoasts. He will lift a signal flag for the nations; he will gather Israel's dispersed people and assemble Judah's scattered people from the four corners of the earth (Isaiah 11:10-12 NET).

With this banner, or signal flag, raised, the Lord not only destroys His enemies, but He also gathers His scattered people from the four corners of the earth.

Therefore, some commentators conclude that the "sign of the Son of Man" is some type of visible sign that indicates the beginning of Jesus' return to the earth.

At His return, He will destroy the enemies of Israel, as well as regather the dispersed people of the nation from the four corners of the earth.

OPTION 2: THE SIGN IS THE CROSS

Others have suggested that the sign is a cross in the sky. This would cause the people on earth to immediately recognize that it is Christ Himself who is returning to the earth. This suggestion was put forward by the early church father John Chrysostom.

OPTION 3: THE SIGN IS JESUS HIMSELF

A third view is that the "sign of the Son of Man" is the Son of Man Himself! This view sees the rest of the verse emphasizing that it is the coming of the Son of Man Himself that causes the mourning of the people of earth. In other words, when the world visibly sees the Lord, they see the sign.

THE RESULT

The appearance of this sign will cause the people of the earth to mourn. This alludes to two Old Testament passages. We read the following in the Book of Daniel:

> In my vision at night I looked, and there before me was one like a son of man, coming with the clouds of heaven. He approached the Ancient of Days and was led into his presence. He was given authority, glory and sovereign power; all nations and peoples of every language worshiped him. His dominion is an everlasting dominion that will not pass away, and his kingdom is one that will never be destroyed (Daniel 7:13-15 NIV).

We also read in Zechariah:

> Then I will pour out a spirit of grace and prayer on the family of David and on the people of Jerusalem. They will look on me whom they have pierced and mourn for him as for an only son. They will grieve bitterly for him as for a firstborn son who has died (Zechariah 12:10 NLT).

In sum, the sign of the Son of Man is some type of visible sign that will appear when the Lord Jesus returns to the earth. It may be some type of banner, or the sign may simply be Christ Himself.

Whatever the case may be, when Jesus Christ returns it will be obvious to everyone on the planet!

The Second Coming of Jesus Christ
(Revelation 19:11-21)

The hope of Christians for the past two thousand years has been the Second Coming of Jesus Christ to the earth. In the Book of Revelation, the Scripture records His actual return. John wrote:

> Then I saw heaven opened, and a white horse was standing there. Its rider was named Faithful and True, for he judges fairly and wages a righteous war. His eyes were like flames of fire, and on his head were many crowns. A name was written on him that no one understood except himself. He wore a robe dipped in blood, and his title was the Word of God. The armies of heaven, dressed in the finest of pure white linen, followed him on white horses. From his mouth came a sharp sword to strike down the nations. He will rule them with an iron rod. He will release the fierce wrath of God, the Almighty, like juice flowing from a winepress. On his robe at his thigh was written this title: King of all kings and Lord of all lords (Revelation 19:11-16 NLT).

As He returns, the first beast, the Final Antichrist, will attempt to make war with the Lord. Scripture speaks of this feeble attempt:

> Then I saw the beast and the kings of the earth and their armies gathered together to make war against the rider on the horse and his army (Revelation 19:19 NIV).

All of this is in preparation for the final battle against Israel—Armageddon (Event 25 and 30).

The carnage of this battle is unimaginable. Scripture explains it this way:

> So the angel swung his sickle on the earth and loaded the grapes into the great winepress of God's wrath. And the grapes were trodden in the winepress outside the city, and blood flowed from the winepress in a stream about 180 miles long and as high as a horse's bridle (Revelation 14:19-20 NLT).

Such is the punishment for those who do not place their faith in the Lord.

There are a number of other things about the Second Coming of Christ which all believers should understand. They are as follows:

JESUS PROMISED TO RETURN

To begin with, it is Jesus Himself who promised to return to earth. On the night of His betrayal, Christ said the following:

> Let not your hearts be troubled. Believe in God; believe also in me. In my Father's house are many rooms. If it were not so, would I have told you that I go to prepare a place for you? And if I go and prepare a place for you, I will come again and will take you to myself, that where I am you may be also (John 14:1-3 ESV).

Since the Lord always keeps His promises, we know that someday He will return to our world.

HE WILL RETURN PHYSICALLY

It is important to note that the Second Coming of Jesus Christ is a physical return to the earth. Scripture compares it to His ascension into heaven:

And when he had said these things, as they were looking on, he was lifted up, and a cloud took him out of their sight. And while they were gazing into heaven as he went, behold, two men stood by them in white robes, and said, "Men of Galilee, why do you stand looking into heaven? This Jesus, who was taken up from you into heaven, will come in the same way as you saw him go into heaven" (Acts 1:9-11 ESV).

As Jesus physically ascended to heaven, so He will physically return to the earth.

This physical return of Christ to the Mount of Olives will fulfill an Old Testament prophecy:

On that day his feet shall stand on the Mount of Olives that lies before Jerusalem on the east, and the Mount of Olives shall be split in two from east to west by a very wide valley, so that one half of the Mount shall move northward, and the other half southward (Zechariah 14:14 ESV).

Hence, whenever the Bible speaks of Christ coming again it always is a physical return that is predicted. In other words, Scripture knows no such thing of Christ merely "spiritually" returning to the earth.

HIS RETURN WILL BE VISIBLE: EVERYONE IN THE WORLD WILL SEE IT

Not only will Christ physically return to the earth, His Second Coming will also be visible to everyone in the world:

Look, he is coming with the clouds," and "every eye will see him, even those who pierced him"; and all peoples on earth "will mourn because of him." So shall it be! Amen (Revelation 1:7 NIV).

Jesus Himself emphasized this:

Then will appear in heaven the sign of the Son of Man, and then all the tribes of the earth will mourn, and they will see the Son of Man coming on the clouds of heaven with power and great glory (Matthew 24:30 ESV).

There is no doubt whatsoever that Scripture portrays the Lord Jesus returning to the earth both bodily and visibly.

THE ASSURANCE THAT IT WILL TAKE PLACE

In fact, the last Book of the Bible ends with the following promise of Jesus:

He who is the faithful witness to all these things says, "Yes, I am coming soon!" Amen! Come, Lord Jesus! (Revelation 22:20 NLT).

In sum, the Second Coming of Jesus Christ to the earth is both personal and visible. This is the consistent teaching of Scripture.

Satan Is Bound for a Thousand Years (Revelation 20)

When the Lord Jesus returns to the earth, one of the things that will take place is the binding of Satan. Scripture explains it this way:

> And I saw an angel coming down out of heaven, having the key to the Abyss and holding in his hand a great chain. He seized the dragon, that ancient serpent, who is the devil, or Satan, and bound him for a thousand years. He threw him into the Abyss, and locked and sealed it over him, to keep him from deceiving the nations anymore until the thousand years were ended. After that, he must be set free for a short time (Revelation 20:1-4 NIV).

There are a number of things that we learn from this passage.

GOD SENDS AN ANGEL TO SEIZE THE DEVIL

The Bible says that angels are created beings, messengers that the Lord uses in His service:

> Of the angels he says, "He makes his angels winds, and his ministers a flame of fire" . . . And to which of the angels has he ever said, "Sit at my right hand until I make your enemies a footstool for your feet"? Are they not all ministering spirits sent out to serve for the sake of those who are to inherit salvation? (Hebrews 1:7,13,14 ESV).

Satan, on the other hand, was an anointed cherub. His authority was higher than that of the angels. However, when he rebelled against God, his destiny was forever sealed.

THE DEVIL IS BOUND IN THE ABYSS

In contrast to the two evil human personages—the beast and the false prophet—the devil will not be thrown into the lake of fire at this time. Instead he will be imprisoned in the "abyss." There is no way for him to escape from this "bottomless pit."

HE WILL NOT BE ABLE TO DECEIVE THE NATIONS

While in prison, Satan will have no ability to deceive the people of the earth. He is kept from having any influence whatsoever.

THERE IS A FIXED TIME TO HIS IMPRISONMENT

It will be for one thousand years that this evil being, the devil, will be kept in prison. Therefore, for this time frame, it will be impossible for him to escape or to have any influence over those living upon the earth.

THERE WILL BE A SHORT TIME WHEN HE IS SET FREE

Finally, his imprisonment in the bottomless pit will end. Instead of being sent to the lake of fire, as was the destiny of the beast and the false prophet, the devil will be set free for a short period of time. Scripture says that this release is "necessary."

Why is this necessary? We will examine this question later as we look at other coming events which the Bible predicts will take place.

The Judgement Upon the Beast and the False Prophet (Revelation 19:20)

In the last days, Scripture tells us that there will be two human beings, the beast and the false prophet, who will bring massive devastation upon the world during the time of the Great Tribulation. The Bible says that they will be punished when the Lord returns:

> Now the beast was seized, and along with him the false prophet who had performed the signs on his behalf—signs by which he deceived those who had received the mark of the beast and those who worshiped his image. Both of them were thrown alive into the lake of fire burning with sulfur (Revelation 19:20 NET).

The end to the beast, the final Antichrist, was predicted long ago. We first read about it in Daniel. It says:

> I looked then because of the sound of the great words that the horn was speaking. And as I looked, the beast was killed, and its body destroyed and given over to be burned with fire (Daniel 7:11 ESV).

THE BEAST ATTEMPTS TO FIGHT THE LORD HIMSELF

The beast foolishly attempts to fight the Lord Jesus, the rider on the horse, as He returns to the earth with His saints. The Book of Revelation explains it this way:

> And I saw the beast and the kings of the earth with their armies gathered to make war against him who was sitting on the horse and against his army (Revelation 19:19 ESV).

As can be imagined, this will be a one-sided battle.

His end is also recorded in the book of Revelation. The Bible says the following about his demise:

> Now the beast was seized, and along with him the false prophet who had performed the signs on his behalf signs by which he deceived those who had received the mark of the beast and those who worshiped his image. Both of them were thrown alive into the lake of fire burning with sulfur (Revelation 19:20 NET).

There is an important thing that we should observe about this punishment.

THE LAKE OF FIRE IS NOT ANNIHILATION

This "lake of fire" will not annihilate the beast or the false prophet. Indeed, one thousand years later, when the devil is thrown into the lake of fire, the beast and the false prophet are still there.

> And the devil, who deceived them, was thrown into the lake of burning sulfur, where the beast and the false prophet had been thrown. They will be tormented day and night for ever and ever (Revelation 20:10 NIV).

While the beast, who is the final Antichrist, and false prophet are still in the lake of fire after one thousand years, they have not been annihilated. Indeed, we should note that the Bible says that "they" will be tormented day and night forever. In other words, when Satan is thrown into this same fiery lake, the beast and the false prophet have already been tormented; and, along with the devil, they will continue to be tormented forever. Such is the inglorious future for these three personages.

The Judgement of the Nations
(Matthew 25:31-46)

When Jesus Christ returns to the earth at His Second Coming, He will return in judgment. Jesus Himself spoke of this coming judgment as He concluded His last discourse to His disciples. His words are recorded in Matthew 25:31-46. They read, in part, as follows:

> When the Son of Man comes in his glory, and all the angels with him, then he will sit on his glorious throne. Before him will be gathered all the nations, and he will separate people one from another as a shepherd separates the sheep from the goats. And he will place the sheep on his right, but the goats on the left. Then the King will say to those on his right, 'Come, you who are blessed by my Father, inherit the kingdom prepared for you from the foundation of the world.' . . . Then he will say to those on his left, 'Depart from me, you cursed, into the eternal fire prepared for the devil and his angels. And these will go away into eternal punishment, but the righteous into eternal life (Matthew 25:31-34,41,46 ESV).

From the Scripture, we read that the kingdom awaits the righteous while punishment is the destiny of the unbeliever.

The Apostle Paul also taught this truth—Jesus will judge humanity when He returns. He wrote the following words to the Thessalonians:

> And God will provide rest for you who are being persecuted and also for us when the Lord Jesus appears from heaven. He will come with his mighty angels, in flaming fire, bringing judgment on those who don't know God and on those who refuse to obey the Good News of our Lord Jesus. They will be punished with everlasting destruction, forever separated from the Lord and from his glorious power (2 Thessalonians 1:7-9 NLT).

The Second Coming of Jesus Christ will be a time of relief, or rest, for believers, and vengeance upon unbelievers. Scripture makes this clear.

This brings up a number of important issues. Whom will Jesus Christ judge when He returns to the earth? Who will enter His promised kingdom?

THE PREMILLENNIAL VIEW OF THE FUTURE

We will answer this question according to the premillennial view of the "things to come." After stating the premillennial view, we will summarize other views of these judgments. Put simply, the premillennial view is as follows.

There will be a literal one thousand-year reign of Jesus Christ upon the earth after His Second Coming to our world. Therefore, we find that Jesus returns to earth, "pre," or before, the thousand-year reign, the Millennium, begins. Millennium is the Latin word for "thousand."

In other words, the return of Christ to the earth does not begin the eternal state for humanity. Instead, there will be an intermediate earthly kingdom that will last a thousand years. During this interval, Jesus will rule and reign upon the earth. After the thousand years is over, then the eternal state will begin.

THE LORD WILL RULE FROM JERUSALEM

When Jesus does return, He will fulfill a number of specific promises contained in the Old Testament. For example, Jesus, as the Messiah, will set up an earthly kingdom where He will rule from the city of Jerusalem.

We read the following in the Book of Isaiah:

> This is what Isaiah son of Amoz saw concerning Judah and Jerusalem: In the last days the mountain of the Lord 's temple will be established as the highest of the mountains; it will be exalted above the hills, and all nations will stream to it. Many peoples will come and say, "Come, let us go up to the mountain of the Lord, to the temple of the God of Jacob. He will teach us his ways, so that we may walk in his paths." The law will go out from Zion, the word of the Lord from Jerusalem. He will judge between the nations and will settle disputes for many peoples. They will beat their swords into plowshares and their spears into pruning hooks. Nation will not take up sword against nation, nor will they train for war anymore (Isaiah 2:1-5 NIV).

This is similar to a number of promises made to the nation of Israel. The Lord will rule in righteousness for one thousand years with Jerusalem as His headquarters.

THE LAST JUDGMENT

At the end of this thousand-year reign of the Messiah, there will be the Last Judgment. At that time, all the unbelieving dead who have ever lived will be judged.

After this event occurs, the Lord will create a new heaven and new earth. This will be inhabited by believers only. For all eternity, believers will enjoy the wonder of His presence! This sums up the premillennial view of future events.

WHO WILL BE JUDGED WHEN CHRIST RETURNS ACCORDING TO THE PREMILLENNIAL VIEW?

According to the premillennial view, there will be four separate groups of people whom the Lord will judge when He returns to the earth.

1. THOSE LIVING FROM THE NATION ISRAEL

2. THE GENTILE NATIONS

3. THE OLD TESTAMENT SAINTS

4. THE TRIBULATION SAINTS

The church, the body of Christ, will have already been judged and rewarded before Jesus returns to the earth. This takes place at the "judgment seat of Christ," also called the "judgment seat of God" (see Event 3). These believers will return with Christ at His Second Coming and will rule and reign with Him during His earthly kingdom and beyond.

The Bible has the following to say about those who will be judged at His Second Coming.

GROUP 1 THE LIVING FROM ISRAEL

When Jesus Christ returns to the earth in triumph, He will judge those from the nation of Israel who have survived the Great Tribulation. This judgment is described in Ezekiel:

> With might and fury I will bring you out from the lands where you are scattered. I will bring you into the wilderness of the nations, and there I will judge you face to face. I will judge you there just as I did your ancestors in the wilderness after bringing them out of Egypt, says the Sovereign LORD. I will count you carefully and hold you to the terms of the covenant. I will purge you of all those who rebel and sin against me. I will bring them out of the countries where they are in exile, but they will never enter the land of Israel. And when that happens, you will know that I am the LORD (Ezekiel 20:34-38 NLT).

This judgment will purge out the rebels from among the nation. The non-rebellious will be the ones entering the kingdom.

Jesus also illustrated this judgment in Matthew 25:1-30 in the parables of the ten maidens and the ten talents. This judgment will be a separation of the "saved and the lost" of those from Israel. We can note the following:

A. THEY WILL BE REGATHERED FROM ALL OVER THE WORLD

These survivors of the Great Tribulation will be re-gathered from all over the world to the land of Israel. This will follow the victory of Christ over His enemies at the War, or campaign, of Armageddon.

B. THE PURPOSE OF THIS JUDGMENT: TO DETERMINE WHOM WILL ENTER THE KINGDOM

Jesus will cause them to "pass under my rod." The purpose is to determine which individuals will enter God's kingdom upon the earth—the Millennium. The righteous from Israel—those who have put their trust in Christ—will enter the kingdom of God. They will experience the long-promised blessings that God has given to that nation. These believers will enter into the millennial kingdom with earthly bodies, not resurrected or glorified bodies.

C. THE UNRIGHTEOUS WILL BE SENT AWAY

However, not everyone will enter the kingdom. The unrighteous from the nation will be purged from the righteous and sent away to punishment. Jesus illustrated this truth in the parable of the talents. He said:

> And throw this good-for-nothing servant into the outer darkness, where there will be weeping and gnashing of teeth (Matthew 25:30 CSB).

They will be banished from the presence of God.

D. THEY WILL AWAIT FINAL JUDGMENT

Although the Scripture does not say, it seems that these people will probably be put to death at that time. Their final judgment does not take place on this occasion. It will most-likely occur after the Millennium—the thousand-year reign of Jesus Christ upon the earth. They, along will all other unbelievers which have ever lived, will be judged and punished at that time.

This briefly sums up what will happen to those from the nation of Israel when Jesus Christ returns. There is a judgment as well as a punishment waiting for them.

GROUP 2 THE LIVING GENTILE NATIONS ARE JUDGED

Jesus spoke of judging the living Gentile (non-Jewish) nations at His Second Coming. Matthew records Jesus saying the following:

> When the Son of Man comes in his glory with all of his angels, he will sit on his royal throne. The people of all nations will be brought before him, and he will separate them, as shepherds separate their sheep from their goats (Matthew 25:31,32 CEV).

Individuals from all the nations will be gathered for judgment at that time.

THOSE SURVIVING THE GREAT TRIBULATION WILL BE JUDGED

These Gentiles are people who are still upon the earth at the end of the Great Tribulation period—the seventieth week of Daniel. This "seventieth week of Daniel" refers to the final seven-year period which the earth will experience before the return of Christ.

These particular Gentiles are the living, not the dead. The dead will be raised for the purpose of judgment in the future. The prophet Isaiah wrote of these people from the Gentile nations in the following manner:

> To the LORD, all nations are merely a drop in a bucket or dust on balance scales; all of the islands are but a handful of sand. The cattle on Lebanon's mountains would not be

enough to offer as a sacrifice to God, and the trees would not be enough for the fire. God thinks of the nations as far less than nothing (Isaiah 40:15-17 CEV).

Everyone who survives this terrible time of tribulation will be judged.

THE PLACE IS STATED: JERUSALEM

They will be brought to the city of Jerusalem and judged in the valley of Jehoshaphat. We read in the Book of Joel:

> "At that time, when I restore the prosperity of Judah and Jerusalem," says the LORD, "I will gather the armies of the world into the valley of Jehoshaphat. There I will judge them for harming my people, for scattering my inheritance among the nations, and for dividing up my land. They cast lots to decide which of my people would be their slaves. They traded young boys for prostitutes and little girls for enough wine to get drunk" (Joel 3:1-3 NLT).

The site of their judgment is certainly appropriate. The city of Jerusalem, the place where Jesus took the penalty of the sins of the world upon Himself at the cross of Calvary, will be the place of God's judgment.

INDIVIDUALS WILL BE JUDGED

While the judgment of these Gentiles is called "the judgment of the nations," it is individuals that will be judged. Many passages speak of this "judgment of nations" as being specific to individuals when Christ returns; some are listed below.

In the parable of the wheat and the weeds Jesus put it this way:

> Let both grow together until the harvest. Then I will tell the harvesters to sort out the weeds and burn them and to put the wheat in the barn (Matthew 13:30 NLT).

Individual judgment is also illustrated in Jesus' parable of the good and the bad fish. Matthew records Jesus saying the following:

> Once again, the kingdom of heaven is like a net that was let down into the lake and caught all kinds of fish. When it was full, the fishermen pulled it up on the shore. Then they sat down and collected the good fish in baskets, but threw the bad away. This is how it will be at the end of the age. The angels will come and separate the wicked from the righteous and throw them into the blazing furnace, where there will be weeping and gnashing of teeth (Matthew 13:47-50 NIV)

Each person, from every Gentile nation, will be answerable to God.

THE RIGHTEOUS ENTER THE KINGDOM: UNBELIEVERS ARE SENT AWAY

The righteous will enter into God's millennial kingdom while the unrighteous will be taken away to judgment. These Gentile unbelievers will be sent to the lake of fire. The King in Jesus' parable declared the following:

> Then the king will say to those on his left, 'Get away from me! God has cursed you! Go into everlasting fire that was prepared for the devil and his angels' (Matthew 25:41 God's Word).

It is not clear if these Gentile unbelievers are immediately sent to the lake of fire or not. Some think these unbelievers are killed at this point, raised later at the Great White Throne judgment, and then sent to the lake of fire.

It could be argued that this is their final judgment so they do not have to appear at the Great White Throne judgment. Therefore, they are immediately thrown into the lake of fire. There is not enough information to be certain.

GROUP 3: THE TRIBULATION SAINTS

Along with these other two groups, there will be people who will put their faith in Jesus Christ during the Great Tribulation period—many of them will be killed. When Christ returns, those who became believers and were killed during this specific period of time, will also be judged. They will be raised from the dead in a resurrected, glorified body, receive rewards, and will enter into the kingdom of God.

In the Book of Revelation, we read the following:

> I saw thrones, and those who sat on them were allowed to judge. Then I saw the souls of those whose heads had been cut off because of their testimony about Jesus and because of the word of God. They had not worshiped the beast or its statue and were not branded on their foreheads or hands. They lived and ruled with Christ for 1,000 years. The rest of the dead did not live until the 1,000 years ended (Revelation 20:4-6 God's Word).

These "souls" are the people who have been beheaded for the testimony of Jesus. They are in a different category from other believers, such as the New Testament church and the Old Testament saints.

GROUP 4 THE OLD TESTAMENT SAINTS

There will also be a judgment of the Old Testament saints. This refers to people who lived during the Old Testament period and trusted the Lord— the God of Israel. They will be raised from the dead and judged. Daniel wrote:

> Many of those who lie dead in the ground will rise from death. Some of them will be given eternal life, and others will receive nothing but eternal shame and disgrace (Daniel 12:2 CEV).

While Daniel speaks of both the saved and the lost being raised, it seems that only the Old Testament saints are raised at this time. The unbelievers from the Old Testament period will be raised and judged at the Great White Throne judgment.

The promise of judgment found here in the Book of Daniel is only a general statement of judgment for the saved and the lost. In other words, he does not specify if they are judged together or separate.

Jesus also spoke of this judgment. Matthew records Him saying:

> For I, the Son of Man, will come in the glory of my Father with his angels and will judge all people according to their deeds (Matthew 16:27 NLT).

These believers, who lived during the Old Testament period, will experience God's rewards.

THERE ARE THOSE WHO HAVE A DIFFERENT VIEW

It is important to note that this view of the judgment to come is not shared by every Bible-believer. We need to make the following observations about other perspectives.

NOT EVERYONE BELIEVES IN A SEPARATE JUDGMENT

Not every Christian believes in a separate judgment of the nations from the Great White Throne judgment. They see only one final judgment at the end of time. In other words, there will be a "Judgment Day." Everything will take place on this one particular day.

NOT ALL AGREE ON THE EXISTENCE OF A LITERAL MILLENNIUM

Those who hold the view of only one final judgment are not in agreement with respect to the existence of the subject of the Millennium—the thousand-year rule of Jesus Christ upon the earth. Some believe that a literal Millennium will occur while others do not. The views can be simply stated as follows:

VIEW 1: THERE IS ONE GENERAL JUDGMENT WHEN CHRIST RETURNS

There are many Christians who do not believe in a literal Millennium. They see only one general resurrection at the time of the Second Coming of Christ. All people who have ever been born, both the righteous and unrighteous, will be raised and then judged at this final judgment. There will be no separate judgment of the saved and the lost. In other words, there will be no intermediate earthly kingdom upon the return of Christ. Eternity will begin immediately after the "day of judgment."

VIEW 2: THERE IS ONE GENERAL JUDGMENT AFTER A LITERAL MILLENNIUM

There are others who do believe in a literal Millennium, but see only one judgment at the end of this thousand-year period. They believe that there will be no judgment before Christ comes or even when He comes again. It is only *after* the thousand-year period of the Millennium that everyone, from the beginning of time, will be judged.

ALL BELIEVERS AGREE THAT ALL HUMANITY WILL BE JUDGED BY GOD

Regardless of these different views, all Christians agree that everyone, both the righteous and unrighteous, will be judged by God in the future. The righteous will go away into eternal life while the unrighteous will be eternally separated from God. The only difference among Bible-believers is the timing of these judgments, not the fact of these judgments. The coming judgment is certain!

IMPLICATIONS FOR THE TIMING OF THE RAPTURE OF THE CHURCH

Although the specific question of whether Jesus Christ will come for His church before the tribulation—the pre-tribulational view—or at the time of His Second Coming to earth—the post-tribulational view—is not dealt with in this passage, the implications are clearly in favor of the pre-tribulational viewpoint.

If the rapture of the church occurs while Christ is coming from heaven to earth at His Second Coming to set up His kingdom, and the church meets the Lord in the air, it is obvious that this very act would separate all the saved from the unsaved.

Under these circumstances, no judgment of the nations would be necessary subsequent to the Second Coming of Christ, because the sheep and the goats would already be separated.

This sums up the various judgments which are to come.

The Restoration of Israel
(Isaiah 11:11, 12, Matthew 24:30, 31)

In our previous volume, *25 Signs We Are Near the End*, we mentioned that the return of the nation Israel to their land in the "last days" would be accomplished in two stages. The first has already taken place when the modern state of Israel was formed in 1948.

However, there will be a second phase to this return which will take place after the Second Coming of Jesus Christ.

Indeed, the people from the nation of Israel will be completely restored to their ancient homeland after the Lord Jesus comes again. The evidence is found in a passage in Isaiah:

> In that day the Lord will reach out his hand a second time to reclaim the surviving remnant of his people from Assyria, from Lower Egypt, from Upper Egypt, from Cush, from Elam, from Babylonia, from Hamath and from the islands of the Mediterranean. He will raise a banner for the nations and gather the exiles of Israel; he will assemble the scattered people of Judah from the four quarters of the earth (Isaiah 11:11,12, NIV).

The New Testament also records this miraculous event:

> Then the sign of the Son of Man will appear in heaven, and all the tribes of the earth will mourn. They will see the Son of

Man arriving on the clouds of heaven with power and great glory. And he will send his angels with a loud trumpet blast, and they will gather his elect from the four winds, from one end of heaven to the other (Matthew 24:30,31 NET).

The Lord, as always, will be true to His promises; the promises made to Abraham, Isaac and Jacob, will be fulfilled. Their descendants will live in the Land of Promise with its well-defined borders. All the nations of the world will come to Jerusalem—the city of the Great King.

THE CHRONOLOGY

Simply stated, the chronology of these coming events is as follows:

First, there is the return of Israel to their ancestral homeland. This has already been accomplished.

Next, the final seven-year period of the Great Tribulation. This is also known as the "Seventieth week of Daniel" and the "Time of Jacob's trouble."

Then, during the last part of this Great Tribulation period, Israel will experience the final siege of Jerusalem. When everything seems to be lost, the Lord will then intervene for His people.

The people of Israel will then repent of their sin of rejecting Jesus as the Messiah.

Christ then returns to the Mount of Olives in the city of Jerusalem.

The Lord then gathers the remnant of His people from the four corners of the earth.

According to Scripture, this is the future that awaits the descendants of Abraham, Isaac, and Jacob.

The Restitution of All Things
(Matthew 19:28, Acts 3:19-21)

Scripture speaks of a time when all things will be restored. Indeed, one of the great promises of the Bible is the "restitution of all things."

Jesus spoke of a time when all things will be "renewed:"

> Jesus said to them, "I tell you the truth: In the age when all things are renewed, when the Son of Man sits on his glorious throne, you who have followed me will also sit on twelve thrones, judging the twelve tribes of Israel" (Matthew 19:28 NET).

Peter also spoke to the crowd about this coming event:

> Therefore repent and turn back so that your sins may be wiped out, so that times of refreshing may come from the presence of the Lord, and so that he may send the Messiah appointed for you - that is, Jesus. This one heaven must receive until the time all things are restored, which God declared from times long ago through his holy prophets (Acts 3:19-21 NET).

He called it "the times of refreshing."

WHAT IS THE IDEA BEHIND THESE PROMISES?

Simply stated, this will be the fulfillment of the finished purposes of God which began in the Garden of Eden. While disobedience brought sin and death, as well as separation from God, there will come a time when the results of the Fall will be overturned. In other words, everything will be restored to the Lord's original design. The earth and its inhabitants will undergo a blessed change!

From these two passages, we discover the following eight truths:

1. THERE WILL BE A TIME OF RESTORING

According to the words of Jesus and Peter, there will be a definite time when everything is restored. This refers to bringing things back from a state of disorder and decay to a state of restoration and order.

2. IT WILL EXTEND TO ALL PARTS OF CREATION

This restoration will extend to all parts of creation where the disorder has been felt. This includes the physical restoration as well as the spiritual restoration of all things.

3. THE RESTORATION HAS BEEN A THEME OF THE PROPHETS FROM THE VERY BEGINNING

Immediately after humanity fell into sin and the earth was cursed, God spoke through His prophets about a time when all things would be restored to their original perfection. In other words, it is a continual and constant theme of Scripture.

4. IT WILL TAKE PLACE AT THE RETURN OF JESUS

It is when Jesus Christ returns to the earth that this restoration will occur.

As Peter wrote, Jesus was "appointed beforehand" as the Messiah to the Jews. Though rejected and crucified, He has risen from the dead and proceeded into heaven.

THE REGENERATION CANNOT TAKE PLACE BEFORE HIS RETURN

This leads us to the next point. Peter stated that it is necessary that the Lord would "remain in heaven" *until* the time arrives for the restoring of all things. When that time comes, then God the Father will send Him back to the earth.

IT IS A TIME OF REFRESHING FOR ISRAEL

This period of restoration is associated with the time of "refreshing" which will come upon the nation of Israel. The nation will be brought to spiritual life again after years in decline.

THE TIMES ARE BASED UPON THEIR NATIONAL REPENTANCE

Before this time of refreshing can occur, there must be a national repentance of the nation. Indeed, they must recognize their national crime of killing their Messiah. This confession will take away their sins which will lead the way for the return of Christ and the times of refreshing.

WHEN ISRAEL REPENTS, CHRIST WILL RETURN

Finally, and most importantly, it is only when this national repentance takes place that the Messiah—Jesus— will return to the earth. At that time, every vestige of the original curse will be removed. "All things" will be made new!

This sums up the promises of Scripture as to the future of our planet as well as to the people who have trusted in the God of the Bible. The "restoration of all things" is indeed coming!

EVENT 40

The Beginning of the Millennium
(Revelation 20:4-6)

After the Lord returns, and judges those who are still alive upon the earth, the one-thousand-year kingdom age will begin. This is known as "the Millennium," which is Latin for "one thousand." Scripture explains this period as follows:

> I saw thrones on which were seated those who had been given authority to judge. And I saw the souls of those who had been beheaded because of their testimony about Jesus and because of the word of God. They had not worshiped the beast or its image and had not received its mark on their foreheads or their hands. They came to life and reigned with Christ a thousand years. (The rest of the dead did not come to life until the thousand years were ended.) This is the first resurrection. Blessed and holy are those who share in the first resurrection. The second death has no power over them, but they will be priests of God and of Christ and will reign with him for a thousand years (Revelation 20:4-6 NIV).

These verses bring up a number of questions.

HOW SHOULD THIS PASSAGE BE INTERPRETED?

Bible-believing Christians are not in agreement as to how to interpret this passage. Basically, there are three ways in which it is viewed.

AMILLENNIALISTS: THERE IS NO LITERAL MILLENNIUM

There are those who hold to an "amillennial" point of view. Basically, they interpret this passage about the Millennium figuratively. In other words, the term "one thousand years" does not correspond to any specific era of one thousand literal years. Within the amillennial belief system, there are differences of opinion as to what exactly this refers to.

Some teach that it denotes the rule of Christ in the hearts of His people who are presently living upon earth. Thus, it is argued that the Millennium of Revelation Chapter 20 is not a perfect state. In contrast to this, the future messianic kingdom is a perfect state. Therefore, the Millennium of Chapter 20 cannot be the future messianic kingdom, rather it refers to this present age.

Other amillennialists teach that the Millennium of Revelation 20 refers to the rule of Christ over His people "in heaven" throughout eternity.

In sum, whatever their specific interpretation of the thousand years is, all amillennialists agree that Revelation 20 is not speaking of a literal intermediate kingdom that will take place upon the earth.

POSTMILLENNIALISTS

Postmillennialists believe that the return of Jesus Christ will occur *after* the Millennium. As is true with the amillennialists, there are a number of differences among those who hold this viewpoint.

Some postmillennialists believe we should interpret the thousand-year reign of Christ, as recorded in Revelation 20, as figuratively. In other words, it refers to the present age in which we live.

Other postmillennialists believe that the Millennium is a literal one thousand-year period of worldwide peace that is yet future. Yet they believe that this will take place *before* the return of Christ. After this period is over then the Second Coming of Christ will take place.

Postmillennialism has not been very popular since the First World War. Indeed, after the war it has become increasingly clear to most people that the world is not getting better and better but rather worse and worse. While there has certainly been progress in many areas of our existence, it is clear to anyone who is paying attention that worldwide peace, as well as the other conditions of the Millennium that the Old Testament prophets described, will never occur without the direct help of the Lord.

The fact that Postmillennialism teaches that world peace, as well as the predicted biblical conditions of the Millennium upon the earth, will take place *before* the Second Coming of Christ, makes it an unrealistic option.

PREMILLENNIALISM

Premillennialists interpret these verses in Revelation 20 literally. They see it as a description of events that will proceed chronologically. In other words, the Second Coming of Christ will precede His literal earthly millennial reign.

THE PHRASE "A THOUSAND YEARS" IS USED SIX TIMES IN REVELATION 20

In Revelation 20, the Greek phrase translated as "a thousand years" occurs six times (verses 2, 3, 4, 5, 6, 7). Since God revealed that certain events will occur both before and after the thousand-year reign of Christ, we should interpret this number literally.

In point of fact, John specifically located this reign as yet future in this verse. This is a strong argument against interpreting it simply as Christ's present reign in human hearts, or His future reign throughout eternity, as many amillennialists do.

Among those who hold the premillennial view, there are basically two main positions. Historic premillennialists, who are also known as Covenant premillennialists, hold that the Lord will fulfill His promises to Abraham through the "spiritual seed" of Abraham. This includes both Old Testament Israel as well as the New Testament church.

On the other hand, Dispensational premillennialists believe that the Lord will fulfill His promises to Abraham through his physical seed—the literal offspring of Abraham, Isaac, and Jacob.

> The earthly reign of Christ will be the literal fulfillment of many Old Testament prophecies. God promised King David that one of his descendants would reign over the nation of Israel forever (2 Samuel 7:10-16).

Dispensationalists believe that this reign will begin after Christ returns to the earth, at His Second Coming. His rule will continue throughout the Millennium, as well as forever into eternity. Since the kingdom of David, and his successors, ruled in an earthly kingdom, the future fulfillment of the promised Davidic kingdom will also take place on the earth.

PROGRESSIVE DISPENSATIONALISTS

Progressive dispensationalists have a different viewpoint. They believe that the rule of Jesus as the successor of David began when He ascended into heaven, after His resurrection from the dead. This rule moves from heaven to earth at the time of His Second Coming and it will continue throughout all of eternity.

Progressive Dispensationalists see the promised kingdom of David as having both a heavenly and an earthly stage. It is often described as already/not yet. In other words, the kingdom in one sense is "already" taking place in heaven, but "not yet" upon the earth.

In sum, most dispensationalists believe that some form of the kingdom of God is currently taking place. They differ as to whether the present form of the kingdom—the church—is an actual stage of the Davidic Kingdom, or distinct from it.

THE PROMISES TO THE OVERCOMERS WILL BE FULFILLED

In Revelation Chapters 2 and 3, in His letters to the seven churches, the Lord made a number of promises to those who "overcome." We find that many of these specific promises will be fulfilled in a literal Millennium.

Among other things, these passages indicate that the rewards that believers receive from the Lord at the judgment seat, the bema, will involve serving under Him in the Millennium.

WHAT WILL LIFE BE LIKE DURING THE MILLENNIUM?

Interestingly, the Book of Revelation gives us no specific information as to what life will be like upon the earth during the Millennium. To discover this, we must go to the Old Testament and the various predictions which are given.

In sum, the Millennium, the literal thousand-year reign of Jesus Christ upon the earth, will follow His Second Coming.

The Resurrection of the Rest of the Believing Dead: The First Resurrection (Revelation 20:5)

Scripture speaks of two distinct resurrections—that of the just and that of the unjust. All Bible believers agree that there will be a resurrection of both the believing and unbelieving dead.

THERE IS A RESURRECTION OF THE RIGHTEOUS

The resurrection of the righteous is described in Scripture in the following ways:

1. THE AWAKENING TO EVERLASTING LIFE

Some of the dead, those who sleep in the dust, will awake to everlasting life. The prophet Daniel wrote:

MULTITUDES WHO SLEEP IN THE DUST OF THE EARTH WILL AWAKE: SOME TO EVERLASTING LIFE . . . (DANIEL 12:2 NIV).

The bodies of the dead, while presently sleeping in the graves, will be awakened someday. This is one way in which the resurrection is described.

2. THE RESURRECTION OF THE RIGHTEOUS

The Bible also says the believers will be raised at the "resurrection of the righteous." Jesus spoke of this time. He said:

> But when you give a banquet, invite the poor, the crippled, the lame, the blind, and you will be blessed. Although they cannot repay you, you will be repaid at the resurrection of the righteous (Luke 14:13,14 NIV).

There will be a resurrection of those who are righteous—those who have placed their faith in the God of Scripture.

3. THE RESURRECTION OF LIFE

Jesus also spoke of the resurrection "of life" or a resurrection "which leads to life." We read of this in John's gospel:

> Do not be amazed at this, because a time is coming when all who are in the graves will hear his voice and come out — those who have done good things, to the resurrection of life . . . (John 5:28,29 CSB).

There is a resurrection of the dead which will lead to eternal life.

4. THE BETTER RESURRECTION

The writer to the Hebrews wrote of a "better" resurrection. He put it this way:

> Women received back their dead, raised to life again. There were others who were tortured, refusing to be released so that they might gain an even better resurrection (Hebrews 11:35 NIV).

Those who believe in the Lord can look forward to this "better resurrection."

5. THE FIRST RESURRECTION

The Apostle John said that after the Second Coming of Christ there will be a "first resurrection." We read of this in the Book of Revelation:

Then I saw thrones, and people seated on them who were given authority to judge. I also saw the souls of those who had been beheaded because of their testimony about Jesus and because of the word of God, who had not worshiped the beast or his image, and who had not accepted the mark on their foreheads or their hands. They came to life and reigned with Christ for a thousand years . . . This is the first resurrection (Revelation 20:4-5 CSB).

Only the righteous will take part in this "first resurrection."

The Bible says that all those who have died will someday be raised. However, not everyone will be raised at the same time. Indeed, only those who have died in the faith are part of this "first resurrection."

The Enthronement of the King
(Luke 1:30-33)

Long ago there was a promise that was made by the angel Gabriel to Mary, the Mother of Jesus:

> Then the angel told her: "Do not be afraid, Mary, for you have found favor with God. Now listen: You will conceive and give birth to a son, and you will name him Jesus. He will be great and will be called the Son of the Most High, and the Lord God will give him the throne of his father David. He will reign over the house of Jacob forever, and his kingdom will have no end" (Luke 1:30-33 CSB).

The King, Jesus, will indeed be installed in Jerusalem to rule and reign.

CHRIST RETURNS AS KING OF KINGS

The Bible says that the babe born in Bethlehem will, one day, return as King of Kings and Lord of Lords:

> I saw heaven standing open and there before me was a white horse, whose rider is called Faithful and True. With justice he judges and wages war. His eyes are like blazing fire, and on his head are many crowns. He has a name written on him that no one knows but he himself. He is dressed in a robe dipped in blood, and his name is the Word of God. The

armies of heaven were following him, riding on white horses and dressed in fine linen, white and clean. Coming out of his mouth is a sharp sword with which to strike down the nations. "He will rule them with an iron scepter." He treads the winepress of the fury of the wrath of God Almighty. On his robe and on his thigh he has this name written: king of kings and lord of lords (Revelation 19:11-16 NIV).

Once installed, Jesus Christ will rule and reign from Jerusalem.

In the last days, the mountain of the Lord's house will be the highest of all—the most important place on earth. It will be raised above the other hills, and people from all over the world will stream there to worship.

People from many nations will come and say, "Come, let us go up to the mountain of the Lord, to the house of Jacob's God. There he will teach us his ways, and we will walk in his paths." For the Lord's teaching will go out from Zion; his word will go out from Jerusalem. The Lord will mediate between nations and will settle international disputes. They will hammer their swords into plowshares and their spears into pruning hooks. Nation will no longer fight against nation, nor train for war anymore (Isaiah 2:2-4 NLT).

WHAT A CONTRAST TO HIS FIRST COMING

Lest we forget, at His First Coming, the following words were said either directly to Jesus, or about Him:

When Pilate heard this, he brought Jesus out and sat down on the judge's seat at a place known as the Stone Pavement (which in Aramaic is Gabbatha). It was the day of Preparation of the Passover; it was about noon. "Here is your king," Pilate said to the Jews. But they shouted, "Take him away! Take him away! Crucify him!" "Shall I crucify your king?"

Pilate asked. "We have no king but Caesar," the chief priests answered. Finally Pilate handed him over to them to be crucified (John 19:13-16 NIV).

The true King was rejected by the people. They chose Caesar over Jesus; hence, they yelled at Pilate to crucify Jesus.

While He was on the cross, those who passed by ridiculed Him:

The people passing by shouted abuse, shaking their heads in mockery. "Look at you now!" they yelled at him. "You said you were going to destroy the Temple and rebuild it in three days. Well then, if you are the Son of God, save yourself and come down from the cross!" (Matthew 27:39-40 NLT).

The tragedy of the cross was summed up by John in the saddest verse of the Bible:

He was in the world, and though the world was made through him, the world did not recognize him (John 1:10 NIV)

Betrayed by one of His own, rejected by His people and then crucified, though He never sinned, sums up the response of the people of Israel to the First Coming of Christ.

However, as we have read, He will return—not as the babe in Bethlehem—but as King of Kings and Lord of Lords! In fact, the Bible calls Him the "Lion of the tribe of Judah."

And one of the elders said to me, "Weep no more; behold, the Lion of the tribe of Judah, the Root of David, has conquered, so that he can open the scroll and its seven seals" (Revelation 5:5 ESV).

At the time of His return, Christ will be installed as the rightful King of Israel, as well the King over the entire earth!

The Millennial Temple
(Isaiah 2:2-4, Ezekiel 40-48)

The Bible speaks of two temples that have been built in the past in Jerusalem. The first was built by Solomon based upon the desire of his father David. It was destroyed by the Babylonians in 587 B.C.

The second temple was rebuilt after the return of the exiles from Babylon. King Herod later expanded this second temple. It was destroyed by the Romans in A.D. 70.

The Bible also predicts that two temples are yet to be built.

The first is the "tribulation temple," which will be desecrated by the coming Antichrist. This temple will be built in unbelief of Jesus as the Messiah.

There is another temple coming after that—the "millennial temple". We learn of this future temple from the writings of the prophet Ezekiel.

WHERE THIS MILLENNIAL TEMPLE FITS INTO GOD'S PROGRAM

Ezekiel recorded the promises of God to the people of Israel—that they would be restored to their Promised Land in the "last days" (Chapters 33-39).

The final section of Ezekiel concerns what takes place when the Lord brings His people, Israel, back to their ancestral homeland, as well as certain changes that will be made to the geography of the Holy Land (Chapters 40-48).

Within these chapters of Ezekiel, it is announced both that God would set His sanctuary in the midst of His people at a future time (37:26-28), and what it would look like and how it would function (40-46).

HOPE FOR THE FUTURE

This promise of a future temple would have provided hope for the people who were held captives in Babylon. Indeed, God's plan for them in the future was not captivity, but rather a new age of blessing with the Messiah ruling from His temple in Jerusalem.

> After a brief introduction to the vision that Ezekiel received (40:1-4), the prophet then described this future temple complex (40:5-42:20). After this, he records the return of the Lord to His holy temple (43:1-9). Once this takes place, worship of the Lord will occur in this new temple (43:10-46:24). In addition, changes will take place in the geography of the Promised Land (47-48).

This sums up what these passages tell us about this coming temple. The question, therefore, is this: How are we to interpret these chapters?

There are three basic views as to how to understand them. They are as follows:

OPTION 1. THEY HAVE ALREADY BEEN FULFILLED IN HISTORY

Some commentators believe that Ezekiel's prediction was fulfilled when the exiles returned from Babylon and reestablished themselves in the Promised Land. In other words, the Temple that is revealed in this vision of Ezekiel has already been built in the past.

RESPONSE

The problem with this view is that the details in Ezekiel's vision were not fulfilled in the building of the second temple. In fact, neither the second temple, constructed under the supervision of Zerubbabel, or the later expansion by King Herod, was ever built to the exact specifications found in Ezekiel. Consequently, there has been no literal fulfillment of this prediction.

OPTION 2. FULFILLED SPIRITUALLY

Many commentators interpret this section "spiritually." They claim that it refers either symbolically to the New Testament church, or it is symbolic of a kingdom that is still future. Whatever the case may be, there will never be a literal fulfillment of Ezekiel's predictions.

RESPONSE

There are several things which we can say in response. First, the Bible does not say that the church replaces Israel in God's program. Add to this, to attempt to find some type of meaning for the church in these chapters, with all the myriad of specific details that are given, seems hopeless.

The same holds true for those who believe that it somehow speaks of the greatness of God's future kingdom.

More important, it trivializes the multitude of details that are recorded in these nine chapters. Indeed, the Lord gives us the exact dimensions of the various rooms in the entire temple complex. Furthermore, the Lord made certain that Ezekiel recorded them precisely as given:

> The man said to me, "Son of man, watch closely, listen carefully, and pay attention to everything I show you, for you have been brought here so that I can show it to you. Tell the house of Israel everything you see" (Ezekiel 40:4 NET).

The fact that the Lord commanded the prophet to document *all* of the details is another reason to reject the idea that these nine chapters are merely symbolic.

OPTION 3. THESE CHAPTERS ARE A LITERAL PREDICTION TO BE FULFILLED IN THE FUTURE

This is the best view. These verses are a prediction of what the last Temple will look like. In the future, there will be a literal fulfillment of what the Lord so meticulously told Ezekiel to record.

In sum, these chapters not only reveal a future temple and its worship, they also record certain physical changes that will take place in the Promised Land when Israel dwells there securely during the Millennium, the one–thousand-year reign of Christ upon the earth.

This understanding of the text is consistent with the rest of the book of Ezekiel, as it is with the entirety of Scripture.

EZEKIEL AND REVELATION

Interestingly, the Apostle John makes reference to some of the things described in Ezekiel in connection with his description of the future eternal state. Revelation 21 and 22 describes life on the new earth after our present earth passes away. It appears that some features of this millennial system of worship that Ezekiel describes will continue on into the eternal state.

These are further reasons to believe that this temple that Ezekiel wrote about it a literal building which will be constructed when the Lord returns to the earth.

EVENT 44

The "Losing" of Satan: The Deception of Nations (Revelation 19:20)

The Bible says that at the Second Coming of Jesus Christ to the earth, the beast and the false prophet are thrown into the lake of fire:

> But the beast was taken prisoner, and along with it the false prophet, who had performed the signs in its presence. He deceived those who accepted the mark of the beast and those who worshiped its image with these signs. Both of them were thrown alive into the lake of fire that burns with sulfur (Revelation 19:20 CSB).

This "lake of fire" will be their everlasting punishment.

Satan, the adversary of God, however, will be kept in the abyss, the bottomless pit, until a future time.

SATAN IS RELEASED AT THE END OF THE MILLENNIUM

Furthermore, at the end of the thousand-year reign of Christ upon the earth—the Millennium—we are told that Satan, the adversary, will be "loosed" from his prison in the abyss—the bottomless pit—for one last time:

> Now when the thousand years are finished, Satan will be released from his prison and will go out to deceive the nations at the four corners of the earth . . . (Revelation 20:7,8 NIV).

261

THE BIG QUESTION: WHY?

If this is a prediction of a literal event where the devil is literally released from his place of incarceration and then allowed to deceive those who dwell upon the face of the earth, the big question is "Why?" Why would the Lord allow this to happen?

The Bible does not give us any specific reason as to why the Lord will do this. However, there are a couple of lessons that we learn from this coming event.

THE CONTINUAL EVIL CHARACTER OF SATAN IS EXPOSED

First, we find that after spending one thousand years locked up in the abyss Satan does not change his evil character. Indeed, this wicked creature picks up right where he left off by deceiving those who live upon the earth.

There is a great lesson in this for all of us. At the very beginning of life on the earth this created being, who was originally perfect in all of his ways, arrogantly decided to sin against God. Now, after being incarcerated for one thousand years, instead of humbly asking for some type of forgiveness from the Lord, he continues with his evil ways. In other words, this personage is beyond any type of help or redemption from the Lord.

This is one of the many reasons as to why we should not ever try to humanize Satan. In fact, many people mistakenly want to "pray" for him. We should never do this because we know from the Bible that it will not do any good. Indeed, the Lord has already given us the outcome of his fate in Scripture.

THE HEART OF HUMANS IS WICKED

A second lesson we learn from the "loosing" of Satan concerns the human heart. The Bible describes it as deceitful and desperately wicked:

The human mind is more deceitful than anything else. It is incurably bad. Who can understand it? (Jeremiah 17:9 NET).

As the reign of Christ progresses throughout the thousand years, we find that many will not embrace His Kingly rule over them. Hence, they will not obey Him.

There will be consequences for this disobedience. For one thing, nations which fail to worship the Lord at Jerusalem will have their rain withheld:

But if any of the nations anywhere on earth refuse to go up to Jerusalem to worship the King, the Lord who rules over all, they will get no rain (Zechariah 14:17 NET).

Zechariah described this act of punishment as a plague while, at the same time, giving specific mention to Egypt:

If the Egyptians will not do so, they will get no rain - instead there will be the kind of plague which the Lord inflicts on any nations that do not go up to celebrate the Feast of Tabernacles. (Zechariah 14:18 NET).

All nations, with specific mention of Egypt, will come under the judgment of God should they fail to obey Him:

This will be the punishment of Egypt and of all nations that do not go up to celebrate the Feast of Tabernacles (Zechariah 14:19 NET).

Why Egypt is singled out is not explained. What it does tell us, as we learn elsewhere (Isaiah 19), is that Egypt will still exist as a nation in the millennium as well as be in favor with the Lord.

It is clear that Zechariah is describing the millennium in this passage, Zechariah 14, not the eternal state. The fact that there will exist nations that could potentially rebel against the Lord, and therefore, face His divine judgment, as well as their need for rain, makes this obvious. Indeed, none of this could happen in the eternal realm.

If any ultimate proof was ever needed about the sinfulness of human nature, it is certainly revealed at this juncture. At the end of the Millennium, after Jesus Christ has lovingly ruled over the earth for one thousand years, Satan will be released from the abyss and permitted to lead one last revolt against Him. Although the people of the earth know the character of the Lord, many of them will still decide to rebel against him.

This event is so tragic. These people who have been living under perfect conditions, who have been governed perfectly by the King of Kings—Jesus Christ—nevertheless decide to side with the devil in his rebellion.

Therefore, the "loosing" of Satan at the end of the Millennium teaches us some valuable lessons about this evil personage and well as the darkness of the human heart.

The Last Revolt Against the Lord Twarted: Gog and Magog (Revelation 20:7-9)

Picking up where our last event left off, Satan, the adversary, has been released from his prison in the abyss. He is allowed, for one last time, to deceive the nations and lead a rebellion against the Lord. The Bible describes this event as follows:

> When the thousand years are completed, Satan will be released from his prison and will go out to deceive the nations at the four corners of the earth, Gog and Magog, to gather them for battle. Their number is like the sand of the sea. They came up across the breadth of the earth and surrounded the encampment of the saints, the beloved city. Then fire came down from heaven and consumed them (Revelation 20:7-9 CSB).

There are a number of important things that we learn about this battle.

THE DEVIL RESUMES HIS EVIL WORK

As we saw in the previous event, instead of having a change of heart, Satan will resume his evil work of deceiving the nations. He will attempt to convince them to submit to his authority rather than that of Christ. Incredibly, this wicked being will gather a large army from all parts of the world to fight against the Lord.

WHO ARE THE PEOPLE THAT REBEL?

The people who follow Satan in this rebellion will be those who have not trusted Jesus Christ as their Savior during the Millennium. Even though everyone will know who Jesus Christ is during this one-thousand-year period (Jeremiah 31:33-34), not everyone will trust in Him as Savior.

While only believers will enter the Millennium, they will have children. Consequently, everyone born during that time will need to personally trust Christ in order to have eternal salvation.

To sum up, Jesus Christ permits Satan to assemble an army and encircle His capital city, Jerusalem, at the end of the Millennium. Seemingly, no sooner than this great army of Satan assembles, fire will come down from heaven and destroy this entire group of rebellious individuals.

This is the inglorious end of Satan, the being who, from the very beginning, has attempted to overthrow the throne of God and usurp His authority.

This also puts to rest the often-brought-up theory that human beings, once they are placed in a perfect environment, will willingly serve the Lord who has created them. Even in this ideal situation of the Millennium, countless people will respond to the very first opportunity they have to rebel against the Lord.

There are a number of questions which arise about this last battle.

WHO ARE GOG AND MAGOG?

The identity of "Gog and Magog" has been the subject of much discussion among Bible-believers. In the Book of Ezekiel, the same names are mentioned in a "last days" invasion of Israel. Gog is the title of the ruler, while Magog is the land from where he comes from.

IS THIS THE EZEKIEL 38, 39 INVASION?

There are good Bible commentators that contend that the invasion of Israel recorded in Ezekiel 38,39 is referring to this same event at the end of the Millennium. The obvious reason as to why these two accounts may refer to the same event is that the names Gog and Magog are used in both sections of Scripture.

COMPARING EZEKIEL AND REVELATION

Yet, the differences between the two events make it impossible to view these two passages as describing the same episode. Indeed, this reference to Gog and Magog in Revelation 21 must not be confused with a similar reference in Ezekiel 38 and 39. In fact, there are a number of reasons as to why each passage is referring to a different event.

REASON 1: THERE ARE DIFFERENT MEANINGS FOR THE TERMS GOG AND MAGOG

While the same terms "Gog and Magog" are used in both accounts, they do not mean the same thing. In Ezekiel, Gog is the title of the leader of an invasion of a few specified nations and Magog is a specific land that is north of Israel.

However, in Revelation, Gog and Magog refer to all the nations of the world. Thus, in Ezekiel, the nations come from the same geographical region while in Revelation they come from the four corners of the earth.

REASON 2: THE SETTINGS ARE ENTIRELY DIFFERENT

Beginning in Ezekiel 36, this prophet, Ezekiel, who was exiled to Babylon, predicts the future regathering of the nation of Israel to their ancient homeland. This prediction was to take place in the "last days."

Ezekiel's prediction goes on to say that, after the people of Israel have returned to their land, there would be a future attack on the nation.

This attack, by Gog, would occur after the Jewish people are resettled in their land and living in peace.

Thus, as Ezekiel says, the people will have *recently* come back to their land, after they have been away for a long time, when this battle occurs. At the end of Revelation, Israel will have been in their land for a thousand years, at least.

REASON 3: IN REVELATION, THE LORD IS ALREADY KNOWN TO ALL

There is another huge difference. It is after this invasion recorded in Ezekiel takes place that both the Gentiles and Israel will then know that the Lord is God:

> In this way, I will show my greatness and holiness, and I will make myself known to all the nations of the world. Then they will know that I am the Lord. . . In this way, I will make known my holy name among my people of Israel. I will not let anyone bring shame on it. And the nations, too, will know that I am the Lord, the Holy One of Israel (Ezekiel 38:23; 39:7 NLT).

This is an entirely different scenario than what we find in Revelation. This battle, at the end of Revelation, takes place at the end of the millennial kingdom. There will certainly be no need for Jesus Christ, the Messiah, to come to be known by either the Gentiles or by Israel at this time. Indeed, He has been reigning over the both Israel and the Gentiles for almost 1,000 years!

In sum, Ezekiel 39 says that after God destroys these invading armies, then all the nations will know that the Lord is God. In Revelation, all the nations have already known, for a thousand years, that the Lord is God.

REASON 4: A CLEANUP IN ETERNITY?

In addition, it does not seem to make any sense that there will be a seven-year cleanup of the earth as the eternal state is about to begin:

Then the people in the towns of Israel will go out and pick up your small and large shields, bows and arrows, javelins and spears, and they will use them for fuel. There will be enough to last them seven years! (Ezekiel 39:9 NLT).

Indeed, we are told that after the incident recorded in Revelation 20 takes place, God will judge the wicked dead and then create a new heaven and a new earth. Thus, there will be no need to clean up the old earth.

REASON 5: WHO GATHERS THE ARMY?

In Ezekiel, the leader Gog has the idea to invade Israel, while in Revelation it is Satan who gathers the army.

REASON 6: THERE IS A DIFFERENT GEOGRAPHY FOR THE DESTRUCTION

In Ezekiel, the destruction occurs once they enter the mountains of Israel—the borders of the promised Land. In the account in Revelation, they will surround the city of Jerusalem before the armies are finally destroyed.

CONCLUSION: THESE ARE DIFFERENT EVENTS

In Ezekiel, the setting of the invasion is before the Millennium—premillennial. In Revelation, it is after the Millennium, or post-millennial.

Satan Is Cast Into the Lake of Fire
(Revelation 20:10)

After the final battle of Gog and Magog, the supernatural being who became the devil, the adversary, will be punished once-and-for-all. It will end his inglorious career.

THE CAREER OF SATAN

From the very start, the God of the Bible has predicted the eventual fate of the created spirit-being who became Satan, or the devil. The Scripture informs us of the following:

1. SATAN'S DESTINY WAS ANNOUNCED AT HIS REBELLION

When this particular personage rebelled in heaven, his ultimate destiny was announced. We read the following account in the Book of Ezekiel:

> You traded far and wide. You learned to be violent, and you sinned. So I threw you down from God's mountain in disgrace. The guardian angel forced you out from the fiery stones. You became too proud because of your beauty. You wasted your wisdom because of your greatness. So I threw you to the ground and left you in front of the kings so that they could see you. You dishonored your own holy places because of your many sins and dishonest trade. So I set fire to you to burn you up. I turned you into ashes on the ground

in the presence of all who saw you. All the nations who knew you are horrified because of you. You have come to a terrible end, and you will never exist again (Ezekiel 28:16-19 God's Word).

While this passage initially speaks of the fall of the King of Tyre, the punishments pronounced seem to go beyond this earthly king. Therefore, they are ultimately against Satan, the anointed cherub who became the devil. The destiny of the devil, therefore, was determined at the beginning.

2. THE FATE OF THE SERPENT WAS PREDICTED IN THE GARDEN OF EDEN

In the Garden of Eden, God prophesied the final destiny of Satan in the judgment He pronounced upon the serpent—the snake. We read of this in the third chapter of the Book of Genesis:

From now on, you and the woman will be enemies, and your offspring and her offspring will be enemies. He will crush your head, and you will strike his heel (Genesis 3:15 NLT).

The seed of the woman, who is Jesus Christ, will crush the head of the snake. The judgment upon the snake is ultimately a judgment upon Satan.

3. IT WAS PREDICTED THAT THE SERPENT WILL EAT DUST

It was also predicted that Satan would have to eat dust. This is a prophetic picture of his final degradation. Eating dust carries with it the idea of total defeat. The prophet Micah wrote:

They shall lick the dust like a serpent, like the crawling things of the earth (Micah 7:17 ESV).

There was judgment upon the snake for its part in the temptation of Adam and Eve. This judgment includes what will happen to the devil.

4. AT THE CROSS THE DEVIL WAS DEFEATED

The crushing of the serpent's head was accomplished at the cross. The Bible says the following about the victory of Jesus:

> The one who commits sin is of the devil, for the devil has sinned from the beginning. The Son of God was revealed for this purpose: to destroy the devil's works (1 John 3:8 CSB).

Jesus Christ came into this world to destroy the works of the devil. The devil knows that he has been defeated. It is just a matter of time before his evil work comes to an end.

HE WILL BE THROWN OUT OF HEAVEN

Satan will be kicked out of heaven during the time of the Great Tribulation:

> So that huge dragon—the ancient serpent, the one called the devil and Satan, who deceives the whole world—was thrown down to the earth, and his angels along with him (Revelation 12:9 NET).

6. THE DEVIL WILL BE CONFINED TO THE ABYSS

We also have noted that, after Jesus Christ returns, Satan will be confined to the abyss, the bottomless pit. Scripture says the following in describing this:

> Then I saw an angel coming down from heaven holding the key to the abyss and a great chain in his hand. He seized the dragon, that ancient serpent who is the devil and Satan, and bound him for a thousand years (Revelation 20:1,2 CSB).

He will be confined to the abyss when the Lord Jesus returns for one thousand years.

7. HE WILL ULTIMATELY GO INTO THE LAKE OF FIRE

Eventually, he will spend eternity in the lake of fire. The Bible says the following somber words about his final fate:

> And the devil who deceived them was thrown into the lake of fire and sulfur, where the beast and the false prophet are too, and they will be tormented there day and night forever and ever (Revelation 20:10 NET).

This is his ultimate destination.

In fact, the Lord Jesus said that this particular place was actually created for the devil and his angels. We read the following words:

> Then he will say to those on his left, 'Depart from me, you who are cursed, into the eternal fire prepared for the devil and his angels' (Matthew 25:41 NIV).

This lake of fire will indeed be a righteous punishment for this evil being and the problems which he has caused.

8. HE WILL BE PUNISHED FOREVER

Contrary to popular belief, Satan will not be in charge of hell. There will be no organized sin with him as the leader. Everyone there will be eternally punished, including Satan.

This sums up what the Bible has to say about the final destiny of the devil. It is clear from Scripture that the Lord will eternally punish him for his horrific evil.

The Great White Throne Judgment
(Revelation 20:11-15)

When the Bible speaks of the "Last Judgment," it is not similar to taking a final test to see whether we pass or fail. That type of judgment has already taken place. It occurs in this life. What we do with Jesus Christ in this life determines how we will be judged in the next.

Thus, this "Last Judgment" is the public recognition of decisions long-since made. The Bible tells us about this awesome event.

1. JESUS SAID ALL HUMANITY WILL BE JUDGED

The "Last Judgment" is also known as the "Great White Throne Judgment." Jesus spoke of the eventual judgment of all humanity:

> Don't be so surprised! Indeed, the time is coming when all the dead in their graves will hear the voice of God's Son, and they will rise again. Those who have done good will rise to experience eternal life, and those who have continued in evil will rise to experience judgment (John 5:28, 29 NLT).

As we have just read, there will be a resurrection which leads to life as well as one which leads to condemnation. Everyone, however, will be judged.

In the Old Testament, the prophet Daniel wrote of a judgment that would lead to "everlasting contempt" or "eternal shame and disgrace."

He wrote:

> Many of those who lie dead in the ground will rise from death. Some of them will be given eternal life, and others will receive nothing but eternal shame and disgrace (Daniel 12:2 CEV).

Judgment will come to everyone.

2. JESUS WILL BE THEIR JUDGE

The Bible says that the Lord Jesus Himself will be the Judge. He said:

> Moreover, the Father judges no one, but has entrusted all judgment to the Son . . . And he has given him authority to judge because he is the Son of Man (John 5:22,27).

The claim of Jesus Christ is that He will be the One who will judge humanity.

3. THE PARTICIPANTS AT THE GREAT WHITE THRONE JUDGMENT (THE PREMILLENNIAL VIEW)

Bible-believers are not agreed as to who will participate in the Great White Throne Judgment. According to the premillennial view, there will be four groups of people who will be judged at this particular time. They are as follows:

A. THE UNSAVED DEAD OF ALL TIME

B. SATAN

C. THE FALLEN ANGELS

D. THE MILLENNIAL BELIEVERS

These are the four specific groups which will be judged at this future time.

THE PREMILLENNIAL VIEW SIMPLY STATED

The premillennial view basically says that Christ will return before the Millennium, His thousand-year reign upon the earth. At that time, He sets up an earthly kingdom where He will rule from Jerusalem for one thousand years.

At the end of the thousand years, there will be a final judgment. However, most believers have already been judged long before this time. Their judgment consists not of condemnation, but rather of rewards, and they have been ruling with Christ in His earthly kingdom since. It is only at the end of the thousand years that this final judgment occurs. Most of the participants in this judgment are unbelievers.

With this in mind, we can observe what Scripture says about this final judgment according to the premillennial view.

A. ALL OF WICKED HUMANITY WILL BE JUDGED

The Book of Revelation speaks of a final judgment of all the wicked who have ever lived. After the thousand years of peace upon the earth, there is a final rebellion of Satan that will be stamped out by God. John wrote about this as follows:

> And when the thousand years are ended, Satan will be released from his prison and will come out to deceive the nations that are at the four corners of the earth, Gog and Magog, to gather them for battle; their number is like the sand of the sea. And they marched up over the broad plain of the earth and surrounded the camp of the saints and the beloved city, but fire came down from heaven and consumed them (Revelation 20:7-9 ESV).

After this event, there is a final judgment of the wicked. John also wrote:

> And I saw a great white throne and the one sitting on it. The earth and sky fled from his presence, but they found no

place to hide. I saw the dead, both great and small, standing before God's throne. And the books were opened, including the Book of Life. And the dead were judged according to what they had done, as recorded in the books (Revelation 20:11,12 NLT).

The people judged at the Great White Throne will include all those who have rejected the message of God. They are raised at this final judgment.

The book of Revelation also says that, at the time of this last judgment, death and Hades will give up their dead:

Then the sea gave up the dead that were in it, and death and Hades gave up the dead that were in them; each one was judged according to their works (Revelation 20:13 CSB).

These people are merely called "the dead." No one is named. This is in keeping with the rest of Scripture where the unbelieving dead are unnamed. While they do exist, and are being punished, they are, in one sense, treated as though they did not exist.

B. SATAN WILL BE JUDGED

Satan, the created spirit-being who became the devil, is also judged. The Bible specifies his judgment in the Book of Revelation. It says:

And the devil, who deceived them, was thrown into the lake of burning sulfur, where the beast and the false prophet had been thrown. They will be tormented day and night for ever and ever (Revelation 20:10 NIV).

His punishment occurs at this time.

C. EVIL ANGELS WILL BE JUDGED

Although the Bible does not specifically say that the evil angels will be judged at this time, Jesus said the lake of fire was prepared for them. We read of His words in Matthew where He said:

Then he will also say to those on the left, 'Depart from me, you who are cursed, into the eternal fire prepared for the devil and his angels!' (Matthew 25:41 CSB).

Their punishment will also come, most likely, at the Great White Throne.

D. MILLENNIAL BELIEVERS WILL BE REWARDED

While all people who enter the Millennium will be believers, there will be children born to these people during the one-thousand-year millennial reign of Christ on the earth. Judgment will also take place for these individuals who are born during the millennial period. They will have an opportunity to believe in Christ, or reject Him.

Those who have believed during this period will likely be judged at the Great White Throne. However, their judgment consists of rewards, not punishment. They will enter into God's eternal kingdom.

4. EVERYONE WILL GIVE AN ACCOUNT FOR THEIR BEHAVIOR

At the Great White Throne Judgment, everyone will give an account of their deeds. Jesus spoke of this awesome moment:

I tell you, on the day of judgment people will give account for every careless word they speak (Matthew 12:36 ESV).

Every word ever spoken will be taken into account.

In another place, the Lord said that all secrets will be revealed:

There is nothing covered that won't be uncovered, nothing hidden that won't be made known. Therefore, whatever you have said in the dark will be heard in the light, and what you have whispered in an ear in private rooms will be proclaimed on the housetops (Luke 12:2,3 CSB).

Nothing will be hidden in this judgment.

5. THIS IS JUDGMENT TO THEIR FINAL STATE

The Great White Throne is the "final Judgment." Those who are judged are assigned to their final state. The Bible does not indicate any chance for belief after this last judgment. This is truly an awesome event!

NOTE: NOT EVERYONE BELIEVES IN A LITERAL MILLENNIUM

We should also note that not every Bible-believer accepts the idea that there will be a literal Millennium following the return of Christ. They believe the Great White Throne Judgment occurs when Christ comes again. His return is the "last Judgment" which the Bible speaks about; the one and only judgment for humanity and angels.

Again, we stress the fact that though there are disagreements among Bible-believers over the timing of the Great White Throne Judgment, all agree that it will indeed occur someday.

EVENT 48

The New Heavens and New Earth Created (Revelation 21:1)

After the Last Judgment where all the unbelievers are separated from the believers, Scripture speaks of the Lord creating a "new heaven and a new earth:"

> Then I saw "a new heaven and a new earth," for the first heaven and the first earth had passed away, and there was no longer any sea (Revelation 21:1 NIV).

One of the questions which arises from this section is, "Why?" Why would the Lord destroy this universe which He originally created? The reasons can be simply stated as follows:

First, though this present earth was made for humans to live upon, sin has entered and completely corrupted every aspect of it. This corruption extends to the human race, the animal kingdom and the environment. Everything has been corrupted. This corruption must be reversed. The new heaven and new earth will reverse this present, sinful state of the world.

THE FULFILLMENT OF HIS PROMISES

There is, yet, another reason as to why the Lord will make a new heaven and new earth. It is to fulfill the promises which He has previously made.

DAVID WAS PROMISED A THRONE FOREVER

For example, King David was promised that one of His descendants would rule forever. The Bible records this promise:

> The Lord declares to you that the Lord himself will establish a house for you: When your days are over and you rest with your ancestors, I will raise up your offspring to succeed you, your own flesh and blood, and I will establish his kingdom. He is the one who will build a house for my Name, and I will establish the throne of his kingdom forever. I will be his father, and he will be my son. . . Your house and your kingdom will endure forever before me; your throne will be established forever (2 Samuel 7:11-14,16 NIV).

One particular descendant of David will indeed rule and reign for all eternity, the Lord Jesus.

AN EVERLASTING KINGDOM WILL BE ESTABLISHED

In Daniel, we also read the promise of God of a kingdom which shall never be destroyed:

> In the time of those kings, the God of heaven will set up a kingdom that will never be destroyed, nor will it be left to another people. It will crush all those kingdoms and bring them to an end, but it will itself endure forever (Daniel 2:44 NIV).

God's kingdom will last forever. In these last two chapters of Revelation, we will read of the fulfillment to that promise.

THE LORD PROMISED TO PREPARE A PLACE FOR US

Finally, we have the promise of the Lord Jesus. As He was about to leave this world He promised to prepare a place for believers:

Don't let your hearts be troubled. Trust in God, and trust also in me. There is more than enough room in my Father's home. If this were not so, would I have told you that I am going to prepare a place for you? When everything is ready, I will come and get you, so that you will always be with me where I am (John 14:1-3 NLT).

The following chapters will reveal the place in which the Lord has prepared for us (Event 49). It is our eternal home in the house of the Father.

Therefore, the new earth will see the complete fulfillment of these predictions and promises. The writer to the Hebrews made this clear:

All these people were still living by faith when they died. They did not receive the things promised; they only saw them and welcomed them from a distance, admitting that they were foreigners and strangers on earth. People who say such things show that they are looking for a country of their own. If they had been thinking of the country they had left, they would have had opportunity to return. Instead, they were longing for a better country—a heavenly one. Therefore God is not ashamed to be called their God, for he has prepared a city for them (Hebrews 11:13–16 NIV).

The people of God have been waiting for this "better country," a heavenly city. We will discover that the Living God will indeed create a new universe where only righteousness will dwell. In doing so, He will fulfill the promises made long ago. Indeed, believers will finally have that heavenly city, that "better country," just as the Lord had promised.

Consequently, the final two chapters in the Book of Revelation will reveal the final stage in the Lord's plan of the ages. The Lord God will deliver the human race from this fallen world into a new, incorruptible world which He will create. In doing so, it will fulfill the original intention of the first creation, as well as fulfilling the promises of a future blessing.

THE NEW UNIVERSE (REVELATION 21:1)

John begins by declaring what he saw—a new universe! The old heaven and the old earth are now gone, replaced by all things new. It is new in the sense that it is a "new kind of universe." Indeed, there is a complete transformation of all things. In addition, we discover that the new earth has no sea in it.

This brings up a few questions: Will everything in the old universe be destroyed, including the home of God? What is the relationship between the old universe and the new one? Why is the new earth without the sea?

WILL HEAVEN, GOD'S HOME, PASS AWAY?

We should note that the phrase "the first heaven and the first earth" refers to the visible universe. John certainly did not mean the special abode of God will pass away! The Bible calls this unique place the "third heaven." Paul wrote:

> I know a man in Christ who fourteen years ago (whether in the body or out of the body I do not know, God knows) was caught up to the third heaven (2 Corinthians 12:2 NET).

The third heaven is a description of the place where the Lord dwells in a special way.

In fact, we read that Jesus "passed through the heavens:"

> Therefore since we have a great high priest who has passed through the heavens, Jesus the Son of God, let us hold fast to our confession (Hebrews 4:14 NET).

The first heaven and the second heaven describe the visible universe.

In sum, it is only the present physical universe that will pass away, or cease to exist, when the Lord makes a new heaven and earth. God's home, heaven, will continue to exist.

WHAT IS THE RELATIONSHIP BETWEEN THE OLD EARTH AND NEW EARTH?

What John saw, a new universe, had been promised earlier in Scripture. For example, Peter spoke of the present universe disappearing:

> The day of the Lord's return will surprise us like a thief. The heavens will disappear with a loud noise, and the heat will melt the whole universe. Then the earth and everything on it will be seen for what they are (2 Peter 3:10 CEV).

From the various passages that speak of the renewal of the heaven and the earth, it is not clear what relationship the new will have with the old. Will the old heaven and earth be merely renewed, or will it be entirely replaced? In other words, is this an example of creation out of nothing, as took place in the initial creation of the heaven and earth? Or is it a thorough renovation of the present heaven and earth, with God reconstructing the elements?

THERE IS SOME MYSTERY AS TO HOW THIS WILL HAPPEN

As is the case with the resurrected body of the believer, there is some mystery in this process. What is clear is that the present heaven and earth will pass away in the form that they are presently in, and God will make something new for believers to enjoy with Him.

WILL IT BE IN TWO STAGES?

In this passage, Revelation 21:1, the eternal state is called a "new heaven and a new earth." However, this is not the same thing that Isaiah the prophet was referring to when he wrote about the "new heaven and new earth" (Isaiah 65:17–25). He was speaking of the Millennium, the thousand-year reign of Jesus Christ upon the earth.

We know this because in this passage we find such things as sin and death still existing in Isaiah's description of this new world. In the eternal state, there will be no sin and no death.

Therefore, it seems possible, even likely, that the re-making of the heaven and the earth will take place in two stages, beginning at the Second Coming of Jesus Christ. When the Lord returns to this earth, the world will be made new for His intermediate earthly kingdom, the Millennium. Then, at the end of His thousand-year rule, the entire universe will be made new.

The Holy City: The Arrival of the New Jerusalem (Revelation 21, 22)

As we noted in the previous event, once the old earth passes away, the Lord will establish a new heaven and a new earth—a new universe.

After seeing this "new heaven and new earth," John then described what he saw—the Holy City coming down from heaven:

> And I saw the holy city, new Jerusalem, coming down out of heaven from God, prepared as a bride adorned for her husband (Revelation 21:2 ESV).

Two things are immediately apparent.

First, the adjectives "new" and "holy" distinguish this city from our present world. Indeed, the New Jerusalem will supersede anything and everything that has happened before.

THE TWO JERUSALEM'S CONTRASTED

On the other hand, calling it "Jerusalem" points to a certain continuity between the two cities. Indeed, both the "old" and "new" Jerusalem are cities which are loved by God and have a special place in His dealings with the human race.

In fact, in the Bible, many great events have taken place, and will take place, in the old city of Jerusalem. The greatest of these are the death of God the Son, Jesus Christ, on the cross of Calvary, and His resurrection from the dead.

Therefore, Jerusalem is central to the biblical account of history as the place of our redemption. However, in contrast to the "old" Jerusalem, there will never be any sin or rebellion in the Holy City.

THE BRIDE IS ADORNED TO MEET THE GROOM

The prophet then compares the city to a bride who is adorned to meet the groom. From this verse, Revelation 21:2, we have several issues that need to be addressed.

The first issue concerns the physical relationship of the New Jerusalem to the present earth. The comparison of the city to a bride also brings up a number of questions, one being: Is the church, which is also compared to a bride, the New Jerusalem?

WHAT IS THE PHYSICAL RELATIONSHIP BETWEEN THE NEW JERUSALEM AND THE NEW EARTH?

There have been several explanations about the exact relationship of the New Jerusalem to the new earth. In other words, where will this city be located?

John sees the Holy City, New Jerusalem, coming down out of heaven, prepared as a bride adorned for her husband. The fact that it is never said to land upon the earth leads some to see it as hovering over the new earth.

In fact, there are many who believe that the New Jerusalem could be a satellite city that remains above the new earth.

Others believe that the New Jerusalem will be within the boundaries of the new earth. Exactly where, is not stated.

When looking at what the Scripture says, we find the text does not specifically say the New Jerusalem will come down to the new earth, only that John saw it coming down out of heaven, from God.

However, the fact that the Holy City is said to have a sturdy foundation would seem to imply that it is somewhere upon the new earth.

IS THE NEW JERUSALEM THE NEW TESTAMENT CHURCH?

There have been a number of people who claim that the description of the New Jerusalem, in the Book of Revelation, is actually a description of the New Testament church. The main reason for this belief is the use of the "bride" figure to describe the New Jerusalem. Since the church is also described as a bride, this has led them to conclude that the New Jerusalem is identical with the church.

However, the bride figure in Scripture describes not only the church, but also Israel's relationship with God. The evidence is as follows.

THE BRIDE FIGURE DESCRIBES THE CHURCH

Earlier in the Book of Revelation, we find that the "bride" figure describes believers in an intimate relationship with Christ:

> Let us be glad and rejoice, and let us give honor to him. For the time has come for the wedding feast of the Lamb, and his bride has prepared herself. She has been given the finest of pure white linen to wear. For the fine linen represents the good deeds of God's holy people (Revelation 19:7,8 NLT).

In this passage, the bride, the true believers in Jesus, has prepared herself for the wedding.

The Apostle Paul made this comparison earlier in his letter to the Corinthians:

I'm as protective of you as God is. After all, you're a virgin whom I promised in marriage to one man—Christ (2 Corinthians 11:2 God's Word).

In this illustration, the church is the bride who has been promised in marriage to Christ.

THE OLD TESTAMENT USES THE BRIDE FIGURE WITH GOD AND ISRAEL

The Old Testament also used the "bride" as a figure to describe Israel's relationship to God. We read in Hosea:

I will accept you as my wife forever, and instead of a bride price I will give you justice, fairness, love, kindness, and faithfulness. Then you will truly know who I am (Hosea 2:19,20 CEV).

We find something similar in Isaiah:

Your children will commit themselves to you, O Jerusalem, just as a young man commits himself to his bride. Then God will rejoice over you as a bridegroom rejoices over his bride (Isaiah 62:5 NLT).

The Lord said the following to Jeremiah:

The Lord spoke his word to me, "Go and announce to Jerusalem, This is what the Lord says: I remember the unfailing loyalty of your youth, the love you had for me as a bride. I remember how you followed me into the desert, into a land that couldn't be farmed" (Jeremiah 2:1,2 God's Word).

Does this mean that Israel, the church, and the New Jerusalem are three names of the same entity? The answer is, "No." They are always kept distinct from one another.

However, the New Jerusalem, while a literal city, also represents the people who live in it, the believers in Christ. Therefore, the same term can describe either the city or the inhabitants of the city, depending upon the context.

In addition, we will later discover that the names of the tribes of Israel are written on the gates of the New Jerusalem. This indicates that those believers from Israel will themselves have access to the city.

We will also learn that throughout these two chapters there is a distinction maintained between the church (who is the bride, the wife of the Lamb), the nation of Israel, and the Gentile nations. These three entities are always kept distinct from one another.

To sum up, while the believers in Christ and the city of the New Jerusalem are distinct from one another, the city and its inhabitants can be described by the same term, the "bride."

DEATH, DYING, PAIN, AND TEARS ARE GONE FOREVER!

One of the greatest promises in Scripture is found in Revelation 21.

After Revelation 21, verse two, John stops describing the New Jerusalem. He will now record God's spoken Word which is delivered from His throne.

As we read, twice we find that this attention getting word "behold" is used. As we have mentioned, this word is very important because it signals something vital is about to be said or take place, not to mention, this use of the term is noteworthy because it is one of the few occasions in the Book of Revelation where God Himself speaks.

Indeed, what we have here is one of the greatest verses in the entire Bible: "All things will be made new." The curse that corrupted all things in the Garden of Eden has been finally reversed! The Lord God will bring about an entirely new creation. People will have new bodies, the animal kingdom will be made new, and we will have an entirely new environment. The results of sin will be forever gone.

After making this statement, we have the Lord's command for John to write these things down. Perhaps John was so overwhelmed when he heard the actual voice of God that he forgot to write down the words. We are not told.

However, the reason for writing them down is revealed to us: The words of God are faithful and true!

We find that this is a recurring theme throughout the Bible. The God of the Bible cannot lie. Indeed, at all times, He speaks the truth; therefore, we can always trust His promises.

There will come a time when pain, sorrow, and tears are a thing of the past.

THE TREE OF LIFE (REVELATION 22)

In the New Jerusalem, the heavenly city, there will be the creation of a "tree of life." The Bible explains it in this manner:

> Then the angel showed me the river of the water of life, as clear as crystal, flowing from the throne of God and of the Lamb down the middle of the great street of the city. On each side of the river stood the tree of life, bearing twelve crops of fruit, yielding its fruit every month. And the leaves of the tree are for the healing of the nations (Revelation 22:1,2 NIV)

A pure river of the "water of life" flows from the throne of God and of the Lamb through the middle of the street in the New Jerusalem. On either side of the river grows the tree of life bearing its twelve kinds of fruit. This suggests God's ceaseless provision for every season.

WHAT IS THIS TREE OF LIFE?

The idea of a "tree of life" takes us all the way back to the beginning. The Bible says that God created the tree of life and placed it in the midst of the Garden:

> The Lord God made all sorts of trees grow up from the ground—trees that were beautiful and that produced delicious fruit. In the middle of the garden he placed the tree of life . . . (Genesis 2:9 NLT).

When Adam and Eve disobeyed God and brought sin into the world, they lost all their access to the tree of life. The Bible says the following:

> Then the Lord God said, "Look, the human beings have become like us, knowing both good and evil. What if they reach out, take fruit from the tree of life, and eat it? Then they will live forever!" So the Lord God banished them from the Garden of Eden, and he sent Adam out to cultivate the ground from which he had been made. After sending them out, the Lord God stationed mighty cherubim to the east of the Garden of Eden. And he placed a flaming sword that flashed back and forth to guard the way to the tree of life (Genesis 3:22-24 NLT).

Now, in Revelation 22, we discover that in the eternal city, the New Jerusalem, the residents will once again have access to a "tree of life." And, since there will never be any more sin, this tree will be able to be eaten from for all eternity.

What is important to note about this "tree of life" however, is that instead of producing its fruit seasonally, like we are used to, this tree will perpetually produce its fruit. In fact, it will produce a new crop each month of the year. Therefore, the new earth will constantly be fruitful. This is another illustration of God's blessings in the world to come.

Also, since there will be no moon and no night, there will not be a lunar calendar to mark time. Evidently there will be some other type of method that will define the different months for the inhabitants. We are simply not told how there can be days and months without the cycle of the sun and the moon.

WILL IT BE NECESSARY TO EAT FROM THE TREE OF LIFE?

We noted that eating from the original tree of life in Eden could perpetuate life forever. Some Bible students think that this may also be the function of this "tree of life" in the New Jerusalem as well. In other words, in some unknown sense, it may exist to maintain the immortality of the inhabitants. However, this is only conjecture since nothing specific is said of the necessity of eating from this tree to remain immortal.

IN WHAT SENSE IS THE TREE FOR HEALING?

Since there will be no death in the new world, in what sense are the leaves of the tree for the healing of the nations?

Some Bible students suggest the "healing tree" is referring back to the Millennium. But this does not fit the fact the we are dealing with eternity, not a temporary kingdom upon the earth.

It is contended that the leaves, in some unexplained sense, promote wellbeing. They will provide healing from the conditions of the old creation. In fact, some understand the word "healing" to mean "health-giving." Whether they promote wellbeing literally or symbolically is not clear.

WHO ARE THE NATIONS MENTIONED?

In the eternal state, we find that nations still exist. They are groups of people which are viewed according to their old creation divisions. There will be a literal Millennium that will take place on the earth before the eternal state begins. From this thousand-year period, there will be countless numbers of children born to those who initially enter.

These children will have the same ethnicity as their parents. Therefore, the simple answer to this question seems to be that the nations are the offspring who have trusted Christ during the Great Tribulation period. These people, who were born during the Millennium, have also put their trust in Christ.

Eternity
(Matthew 25:34, Revelation 21:3)

The last of our list of fifty coming events is different from all the rest. Indeed, it is the only one that will never end—Eternity! This is the wonderful promise of Scripture, that those who believe in the God of the Bible will live forever in His presence.

THE PROMISES OF GOD

We will cite a few of many promises that Scripture gives us with respect to our eternal destiny.

The most famous verse in Scripture truly says it all:

> For God loved the world in this way: He gave his one and only Son, so that everyone who believes in him will not perish but have eternal life (John 3:16 CSB).

Those who place their faith in Jesus will indeed have everlasting life.

The Lord will show His greatness to us throughout eternity:

> And God raised us up with Christ and seated us with him in the heavenly realms in Christ Jesus, in order that in the coming ages he might show the incomparable riches of his grace, expressed in his kindness to us in Christ Jesus (Ephesians 2:7 NIV).

Among other things, this shows that our lives in eternity will not be static. In other words, we will continue to see His greatness and the riches of His grace in the coming ages.

THE PROMISE OF DWELLING WITH THE LORD FOREVER

Scripture gives this testimony of what will take place in the future:

> Then I heard a loud voice from the throne: Look, God's dwelling is with humanity, and he will live with them. They will be his peoples, and God himself will be with them and will be their God (Revelation 21:3 CSB).

It is almost overwhelming to think about this. For all eternity, the Lord will dwell with us. We will be His people and He will be our God!

THE RIGHTEOUS WILL INHERIT GOD'S EVERLASTING KINGDOM

Jesus spoke of a time when the righteous, those who have believed in Him, will inherit the kingdom of God.

> Then the King will say to those on his right, 'Come, you who are blessed by my Father; inherit the kingdom prepared for you from the foundation of the world (Matthew 25:34 CSB).

THE GUARANTEE OF JESUS

Finally, at the end of the Book of Revelation, we have this guarantee from Jesus:

> I, Jesus, have sent my angel to attest these things to you for the churches. I am the root and descendant of David, the bright morning star (Revelation 22:16 CSB).

The Lord Jesus attests that the words recorded in the Book of Revelation are true. In other words, the events predicted will indeed come to pass.

Eternity in the presence of the living God, where there is no pain, no suffering, no death, and only joy unspeakable, is the destiny of those who believe in Christ!

Summary and Conclusion to our Three-Book Series

In our series on the subject of Bible prophecy, we have looked at a number of important matters. Briefly, we can summarize them as follows:

BIBLE PROPHECY IS A CENTRAL TEACHING OF SCRIPTURE

The subject of Bible prophecy is not something obscure in the Bible. Indeed, from the first book of the Bible to the last, we have examples of future predictions.

THE ABILITY TO PREDICT THE FUTURE IS THE CLAIM OF SCRIPTURE ITSELF

This leads us to our second point. The claim to be able to accurately predict the future comes from the Bible, itself.

THERE ARE MANY EXAMPLES OF FULFILLED PROPHECY

We also find numerous examples of specific biblical predictions which have been literally fulfilled.

THERE ARE MANY SIGNS THAT ARE PRESENTLY BEING FULFILLED

Many predictions, with respect to the "last days," have either been fulfilled or are in the process of being fulfilled.

CONCLUSION: WE HAVE EVERY RIGHT TO EXPECT THAT ALL PREDICTIONS WILL ULTIMATELY BE FULFILLED

With these facts in mind, we can be confident that these predicted events will indeed be fulfilled at some time in the future.

About the Author

Don Stewart is a graduate of Biola University and Talbot Theological Seminary (with the highest honors).

Don is a best-selling and award-winning author having authored, or co-authored, over seventy books. This includes the best-selling *Answers to Tough Questions*, with Josh McDowell, as well as the award-winning book *Family Handbook of Christian Knowledge: The Bible*. His various writings have been translated into over thirty different languages and have sold over a million copies.

Don has traveled around the world proclaiming and defending the historic Christian faith. He has also taught both Hebrew and Greek at the undergraduate level and Greek at the graduate level.

Books Available by Don Stewart

The following books are now available from Don Stewart in print as well as in digital format. You can find them at our website www.educatingourworld.com, as well as Amazon and iTunes.

The Bible Series

What Everyone Needs to Know about the Bible
10 Reasons to Trust the Bible

The God Series

Does the God of the Bible Exist?
What Everyone Needs to Know About God
God Has Spoken to Us: Are We Listening?
The Trinity

The Jesus Series

The Case for Christianity
Did Jesus Exist? Are the Records about Him Reliable?
What Everyone Needs to Know about Jesus
The Life and Ministry of Jesus Christ

The Holy Spirit Series

What Everyone Needs to Know About the Holy Spirit
How the Holy Spirit Works in Our Lives
Spiritual Gifts: Part 1: What Are Spiritual Gifts? Are all Spiritual Gifts for Today?
Spiritual Gifts: Part 2: What Are the Various Gifts of the Holy Spirit?
Spiritual Gifts: Part 3: Speaking in Tongues
Divine Healing: Does God Heal Everyone?

The Afterlife Series

Living in the Light of Eternity
What Happens One Second After We Die?
Resurrection and Judgment
Heaven
Hell

The Unseen World Series

Angels
Evil Angels, Demons, and the Occult
Satan

The Last Days Series

The Rapture
The Jews, Jerusalem, and the Coming Temple
In Search of the Lost Ark: The Quest for the Ark of the Covenant

Christian Living Series

Living the Christian Life
Winning the Spiritual War

With many more books to come, please check back at our website to discover the latest books we have available.

Made in the USA
Middletown, DE
24 June 2019